The Dignity of Labour

To Anna and Emmett

The Dignity of Labour

Jon Cruddas

polity

First published in 2021 by Polity Press

Polity Press
65 Bridge Street
Cambridge CB2 1UR, UK

Polity Press
101 Station Landing
Suite 300
Medford, MA 02155, USA

ISBN-13: 978-1-5095-4078-5
ISBN-13: 978-1-5095-4079-2 (pb)

A catalogue record for this book is available from the British Library.

Library of Congress Cataloging-in-Publication Data

Names: Cruddas, Jon, author.
Title: The dignity of labour / Jon Cruddas.
Other titles: Dignity of labor
Description: Medford : Polity Press, 2021. | Includes bibliographical
    references and index. | Summary: "The 21st century's greatest
    scholar-politician unpicks the degraded politics of contemporary work
    and advocates an alternative"-- Provided by publisher.
Identifiers: LCCN 2020039536 (print) | LCCN 2020039537 (ebook) | ISBN
    9781509540785 (Hardback) | ISBN 9781509540792 (Paperback) | ISBN
    9781509540808 (ePub)
Subjects: LCSH: Labor--Moral and ethical aspects--Great Britain. |
    Labor--Religious aspects--Catholic Church. | Labour Party (Great
    Britain) | Marxian economics--Great Britain. | Great Britain--Politics
    and government--21st century.
Classification: LCC HD4905.3.G5 C77 2021 (print) | LCC HD4905.3.G5
    (ebook) | DDC 331.01/3--dc23
LC record available at https://lccn.loc.gov/2020039536
LC ebook record available at https://lccn.loc.gov/2020039537

Typeset in 11 on 13 pt Sabon by
Servis Filmsetting Ltd, Stockport, Cheshire
Printed and bound in Great Britain by Short Run Press

For further information on Polity, visit our website:
politybooks.com

Contents

Preface   vi
Acknowledgements   viii
About the Author   x

Prologue   1
1 Work and the Modern World   7

Part I   The Economics of Labour   **29**

2 The Labour Problem   31
3 Miracle Cures   48
4 New Labour   62
5 A Return to Marx   79

Part II   The Ethics of Labour   **95**

6 Dignity   97
7 What Do We Think and What's Going to
     Happen?   117
8 Justice and the Left   130
9 Human Labour and Radical Hope   153
Epilogue   185

Notes   191
Index   211

Preface

Dignity is the type of big word favoured by popes and presidents. For George W. Bush it framed bioethical challenges and Barack Obama the pursuit of international human rights. Pope Francis talks of the irrepressible dignity of every human.

When I was young, I was taught about the dignity of labour. For my devout mother it was part of our Catholic teaching. As a teenage union member, I heard talk of it from the same guy who told me to read *The Ragged Trousered Philanthropists*. It is an unfashionable term that suggests all jobs have worth and status, that no occupation should be considered superior.

Until recently if we discussed dignity, we were likely to be contemplating how we die rather than how we live. The pandemic changed this. In the face of death, we reconsider how we live and what we value in the contribution of others. Personally, I know I did years ago when I had to confront the possibility of my own death.

The pandemic interrupted our work or stopped it altogether and affected how we consider the work of others. We applauded care home workers, nurses, porters, orderlies and doctors. We were moved by the sacrifice of tube, bus and lorry drivers, cleaners, teachers, the police and fire service, front-line council workers – welfare and housing officers, maintenance and refuse operatives – as well as delivery drivers, supermarket employees and many others. These jobs are now more visible and have acquired renewed standing. We recognize the dignity of the labour.

Until recently we were told that many of these jobs would soon be automated and few cared. This work is often poorly rewarded, performed by those considered part of the 'left-behind'. Yet we clapped in appreciation of this labour; these vocations gathered esteem. Yet dignity is not just about status. Something else was going on.

Dignity is elusive, difficult to define, not just about worthiness in a job hierarchy. It is also about something we acknowledge when lost, the negation of dignity, and suggests the violation of an essential humanity. Something that implies intrinsic human worth and acceptable moral standards in terms of rights, freedoms and obligations in the ways people live together.

These are questions of justice. They suggest ethical duties in how we order society to remedy the violation of dignity. When such indignities are recognized and remedied, we confer a certain dignity on ourselves and society. In turn, our inability to confront them – in tolerating forms of death, punishment, slavery, abuse and exploitation – compromises our personal and collective dignity.

In pandemic and death, we recognized the brave selfless contribution of others and challenge ourselves. How we resolve these questions of human dignity will help define how we live together and who we become.

Acknowledgements

Many people have helped with this book. I would like to thank all those that took part in a series of six seminars throughout 2017 at Churchill College, Cambridge, sponsored by the Common Good Foundation: Sam Boyd, Lewis Coyne, Ruth Davis, Stephen Davison, Maurice Glasman, Gwen Griffith-Dickson, Scott Langdon, Lisa Nandy, Adrian Pabst, F.H. Pitts, Jonathan Rutherford, the late Roger Scruton and Ed Wallis. Some of the papers I presented in these seminars inform chapters that follow, and I want to record my appreciation for the invaluable comments and feedback I received.

I am also grateful to the Humanism and Identity Group convened by Jonathan Rutherford that met throughout 2018–19 including Jade Azim, Daniel Chandler, Richard Grayson, Jack Hutchison, Hannah O'Rourke, Adrian Pabst, Tobias Phibbs, Matthew Sowemimo and Florence Sutcliffe-Braithwaite.

I particularly want to thank Peter Nolan and Harry Pitts for supplying detailed comments on the draft of the book and for their encouragement and help in improving the overall argument with their suggestions and criticisms. I must also acknowledge Peter's long-term friendship, guidance and supervision, especially concerning questions of value, productivity and work futures. I am also indebted to Stuart White for sharing materials on Universal Basic Income, to Michael Sandel for conversations over several years on key themes in the book and to Kenneth O. Morgan and John Shepherd for helping me to navigate labour history. I also wish to thank Liam Baker, Torsten Bell, Florence Gildea, Nick Lowles and Carys Roberts for support with some of the empirical data.

I would also like to record my appreciation to the staff and associates of Nuffield College, Oxford, especially for insights into the history of the 'Oxford School', including the participants at a conference entitled '50 Years after the Donovan Commission' organized by the History and Policy Trade Union Forum. I would like to thank Peter Ackers and John Kelly for subsequent conversations and support from the Centre for Sustainable Work and Employment Futures at the University of Leicester.

My editor George Owers has been quite brilliant throughout this project and I genuinely cannot thank him enough as well as everyone at Polity.

I wish to thank my staff and local party for being patient while I worked on this project.

Finally, I owe an enormous debt of gratitude to my constituents in Dagenham and Rainham. Above anything, their knowledge, wisdom and extraordinary resilience inform the pages that follow.

About the Author

Jon Cruddas is the Labour MP for Dagenham and Rainham. He joined the party as a teenager and was active in the Australian Builders Labourers Federation. He studied for an MA and PhD within the Industrial Relations Research Unit at Warwick University.

In 1989 he joined the Labour Party Research Department with responsibility for labour market policy. In 1994 he was transferred into the office of the General Secretary. In 1997 he was appointed the Deputy Political Secretary to Prime Minister Tony Blair working on labour market policy and relations with the unions and TUC. In that period, Labour introduced the National Minimum Wage and a series of initiatives to support union recognition and fairness at work.

In 2001 he was elected as the Labour MP for Dagenham in East London, redesignated Dagenham and Rainham following boundary changes in 2010.

In 2007 he was a candidate for Deputy Leader of the Labour Party. Between 2012 and 2015 he was Policy Coordinator within the Shadow Cabinet of Ed Miliband. He is a Visiting Fellow at Nuffield College, Oxford, and Visiting Professor at the Centre for Sustainable Work and Employment Futures at the University of Leicester.

The joy and moral stimulation of work must no longer be forgotten in the mad chase for evanescent profits.

(Franklin D. Roosevelt, Second Inaugural Address, 20 January 1937)

Prologue

For many of our fellow citizens modern capitalism has failed to deliver. Yet it is the left that lies in crisis. It lacks purpose and energy, expressed in defeat and decay, not least in the epic 2019 election loss. Politically, this reflects the collapse of a post-war social democracy built around growth, welfare capitalism and distributive justice, and the destruction of the telos – the absence of a noticeable conception of the good life.

Progressive politics has sought solace in liberal abstraction, appearing remote and disconnected from the people it seeks to represent. We can account for this crisis historically as representing the long-term victory of economistic and technocratic thinking. Ethical traditions have lost out to utilitarian approaches to justice. Consequently, the left has lost its language and existence in the everyday lives of the people. The task is one of political reimagination achieved by a return to exiled political and philosophical traditions to help re-establish a public philosophy for the left.

In response to this crisis, irrespective of painful collisions with the electorate, many on the left today foresee a strange new utopia, one that will provide liberty through abundance and a workless future powered by automation, machine learning and artificial intelligence (AI). A few years ago, talk was of 'capitalist realism' and a dominant neo-liberal dystopia; now we anticipate a brave new world of 'postcapitalism', even 'fully automated luxury communism'.[1] It is utopian thinking of a type unrecognizable to my East London constituents.

Dagenham is a blue-collar community built to house the labour necessary to propel twentieth-century capitalism. We have relied on this labour at moments of national crisis, in wartime munitions and the production of Bren gun carriers. Most recently, when on 30 March 2020 a consortium of UK industrial, technology and engineering companies came together to produce medical ventilators as the globe was consumed by pandemic, Dagenham was the designated site to physically build the machines to safeguard the health of the nation. Work and Dagenham are synonymous.

. . .

Dagenham is proud of its working-class traditions. In the names of the streets and public buildings, the community respects East London Labour leaders such as George Lansbury and Clement Attlee and union agitators like Jack Jones and Ron Todd.

Its foremost building, the Civic Centre, aka 'the Kremlin', is symbolic of earlier generations' struggles for citizenship and access to justice through slum clearance. The mighty Becontree Estate upholds the virtue of mass public housing and the pre-war advance of working people. Dagenham's Ford plant represents both the twentieth-century mode of production and epic industrial struggles of the past. Yet the more recent story is one of deindustrialization, extraordinary demographic change and struggles against the British National Party, which by 2010 held twelve of the fifty-one local council seats. This shifting history of class and work was dramatized in two recent films.

Nigel Cole's *Made in Dagenham* was nominated for

Outstanding British Film at the 2010 BAFTAs. It is a romantic tale of class solidarity and the fight for equal pay amongst a rehoused post-war generation. It centres on the 187 Ford seamstresses that went on strike in 1968 but received mixed support from within the Labour government. It had a stellar cast including Bob Hoskins as a dodgy union guy, John Sessions playing a lovable Harold Wilson, and Miranda Richardson as feisty minister Barbara Castle.

Andrea Arnold's 2009 *Fish Tank* won the 2009 Cannes Jury Prize. In it a dance-obsessed 15-year-old Mia is chased around her estate by social services. We see plenty of daytime special brew and the parading of weapon dogs – Mia's is named 'Tennents'. Work doesn't feature; it is something only brought in by the lover/father figure outsider. In one scene Mia is bewildered by his payslips; they represent something she cannot comprehend. Family hardly exists. Where it does there is little communion or dialogue. Mother and daughter finally talk, not in words but through dance, as Nas raps 'life's a bitch and then you die'.

The two films were shot within months of each other on the same estate – the Mardyke – in my Dagenham and Rainham constituency.[2] A simple contrast between the films suggests an economic and social transformation driven by changes in employment. It offers a historic arc whereby the hopes and solidarities of an era of mass production and consumption, of Dagenham Fordism, are replaced by the indignities of worklessness, relational disintegration and violence. In one film pride refracts through socialized housing, intergenerational advancement and material progress. In the other it descends into modern isolation, mental decay and nihilism.

One film is awash with dignified possibility, a visual slam dunk of *Full Monty* or *Billy Elliot* working-class nostalgia. Add in some cockney swag and sus and the viewer feels good. It reappeared as a successful West End musical. The other film is a tougher watch. It offers us a modern parable to globalization, economic liberalism and the destruction of family; a dystopia where a once noble class is barely recognizable.

The films act as companion pieces, where political hope journeys towards despair and humiliation in a story refracted through the changing character of work. Their release occurred as the country changed. Both came out months after the 2008 economic crash. By then New Labour was destroyed. 2010 was to be the party's worst defeat since 1918, although worse was to follow five years later. In the late 2000s, Blair was despised by many in his own party. Gordon Brown had shown early prom- ise but was sunk even before Mrs Duffy blindsided him on a Rochdale street in 2010. On release, Arnold's dose of social-realist commentary appeared to fit with David Cameron's talk of 'Broken Britain'. In Dagenham there was anger, best expressed in battles with the far right, but mostly a sense of resignation, loss and abandonment. At the 2010 General Election, BNP leader Nick Griffin believed he would triumph in the neighbouring Barking constituency and his party would take control of the coun- cil the same day.

The political environment of the 1968 of *Made in Dagenham* was very different. Wilson's vision of 'White Heat' was in retreat after 1966 but traditional Labourism was not. Alongside, in the slipstream of Crossland's *The Future of Socialism*, Roy Jenkins was striving to legislate a rights-based equality. 1968 also saw the publication of *The May Day Manifesto* – co-authored by Raymond Williams, E.P. Thompson and Stuart Hall – a radical socialist human- ist counterstatement to Labour policies and practices.

The contrast between the state of the left in 1968 and 2010 is stark. In the late 1960s it was alive and agile, reflected in this active contest between alternative models of justice – the utilitarianism of the economist Harold Wilson, the rights agenda of Labour revisionism, and the ethical concerns of the New Left, the first two battling it out within Cole's 2010 take on retro Labour.

By the time *Fish Tank* hit the screens, the left was running on empty. The Berlin Wall had been down 20 years. European social democracy had surfed a nineties' growth spurt built on debt. The left went all in on the 'Third Way' and the 'end to boom and bust'. By 2008 when the music stopped, it looked little more than a vainglorious punt. Environmentalism was under siege through questionable statistics and the appearance of a manipulated science. The soaring Obama rhetoric had landed around moderate health reform and deepening material injustice. The 2015 election loss was one of the most significant defeats for the left since its organized inception in the 1890s. Then things deteriorated.

Amongst the party membership the election of Jeremy Corbyn provided a virtuous antidote to what had gone before. Many extracted renewed hope from significant seat gains in a 2017 election loss that offset underreported chinks in what was later termed Labour's 'Red Wall'. At best a brittle unease remained between the party and significant sections of the electorate. At worse palpable resentment and anger were clearly on show amongst many the left was created to represent. They were there at the Brexit referendum twelve months earlier and festered in the years of Brexit stasis that followed, before the wall formally collapsed, bringing with it an 80-strong Tory majority in late 2019.

In Dagenham, 70 per cent voted to leave the EU. On election day pollsters assumed a significant Tory victory.[3] We held on, just. We chiselled out a 293 majority by somehow retaining nearly 90 per cent of our support, one of the few bricks that stayed upright in Labour's disintegrating 'Red Wall'. Months later a virus detonated politics, undermined the government and created unanticipated space for a demoralized left under new leadership.

The following chapters navigate this terrain. We focus on the work people do, what it means to them, how this has changed and what might happen in the future following the pandemic. We inspect fashionable visions to overturn the system – new left utopias – fuelled by technological change compared to more prosaic traditional desires to civilize capitalism. Talk of a 'post-work' nirvana sits uncomfortably with traditional attempts to regulate employment and respect the dignity of human labour, especially given the calamitous effects of a tiny virus. We will ask if such modern utopias offer 'radical hope' and help build a new left telos to confront authoritarian populism, or distract with bouts of indulgent scientific fiction, detours symptomatic of a dying political tradition. Throughout we bend the conversation through Dagenham.

1
Work and the Modern World

Politics and Belonging

Political instability threatens the foundations of liberal democracy. We cannot assume democracy will prevail. It requires us to rethink the purpose of politics.

Politics demands thought and action. Thought in asking philosophical questions, such as: how do we wish to live, what provides meaning in our lives, where and to what do we belong? How we answer these questions has helped shape competing theories of justice; visions of how society should be organized. Action in terms of the practice of politics, understood to refer to the way power is exercised on behalf of the people.[1] A practice in which different political traditions contest the governance of a specific community or territory; a competition between groups and shared interests to shape the collective 'we'.

The two elements, thought and action, are linked by the ways the practical contest is often, not always, shaped by these alternative philosophical approaches to justice, grounded within different traditions of thought. Politics addresses our beliefs and attachment to the communities within which we live and might think we belong.

However, today's political instability could reflect a declining attachment to physical communities in the modern world, disrupted by technological change and the processes of globalization. The popular Marxist thinker David Harvey has talked of 'time-space compression' and 'a speed-up in the pace of life, while so overcoming spatial barriers that the world sometimes seems to collapse inwards upon us'.[2] It could also mean the opposite. Such change might threaten our attachments but reassert new, more disruptive forms of community and nation.

Political instability might reflect a declining philosophical attachment to the idea of a political community. Are we attached, for example, to a specific rather than global community? Or in terms recently popularized, are we citizens of somewhere rather than anywhere?[3] Do our concerns tend towards the parochial rather than the cosmopolitan? These questions are difficult ones for practising politicians who seek mandates from specific territories – a constituency or nation – rather than global electorates. Do these politicians have specific moral obligations to their constituents over and above global responsibilities to all inhabitants of the planet?

These practical and philosophical questions challenge a sense of politics grounded within geographical boundaries and emerge at a period of political instability. Do they help account for such political unease or are they symptoms of it? Across the globe democratic politics appears endangered. Just a few years ago mainstream politics assumed it had reached a high point of human evolution achieved through the dominance of the market. A specific form of liberal democratic politics – dominant in the era we now recognize as neo-liberalism – announced it had secured the 'end of history' yet is now upended by the forces of authoritarianism and populism.

The terms of political debate are being redrawn. This book engages with these technological, philosophical and practical political debates through the study of the work we do.[4] We discuss the purpose of work in our lives, if this is changing and how this might affect the lives we wish to live. For instance, if work retains personal significance, what consequences follow when it is threatened and is unable to provide what we wish it would? How do these threats find political expression and how might society respond? We discuss the political implications of alternative ways to understand the physical and mental labour we perform.

Identities based on work are transforming in an age for many characterized by precariousness, declining material reward and flatlining social mobility, digitalization, job rotation and meaningless labour. Many now question the future of work itself. These shifts might alter our views about work and how we understand our own lives, and be expressed in how we live together.

I should make clear from the outset that personally I believe work can be a vocation, a calling, and create significant landmarks in life which provide identity and belonging.[5] The practice of belonging, or dwelling, involves sacrifice and is rewarded in the creation of community. Yet this orthodox approach is unfashionable today, especially on the left. The issues we will address therefore stretch beyond conventional political concerns to maximize utility – of material justice – and direct us towards questions of personal character and attachment.

Degradation

Work is important beyond providing us with material subsistence. It can both contribute to and undermine our overall sense of worth; our human wellbeing. This suggests a basic paradox. Work can be a source of human dignity; it can provide meaning and purpose in our lives and confer a certain standing in the eyes of others. Yet it is not guaranteed to deliver these things. Work can be degrading.

This paradox of labour links to another recurring theme of the book: the contrast between what we want from life and what modern capitalism provides. This simple juxtaposition, between how we might wish to live and how we inhabit the world, found political expression on the streets of Dagenham and in the turbulence engulfing liberal democracy even before the virus struck.

One recent short book has addressed the paradoxical quality of labour in an accessible way. James Bloodworth's popular book *Hired* has helped stimulate public debate about the realities of modern work in places often patronized as 'left behind'.[6] It is a compelling account of life and employment revealed through personal experiences working in a warehouse, at a call centre, as a care worker and as an uber driver. He finds insecurity, ruthless discipline, surveillance, atomization, underpayment and underemployment.

Hired is uplifting in the way it gives voice to the experiences of these workers, yet unsettling when it reveals the collapsing personal esteem associated with the jobs people are hired to do. The book also captures a deeper story. It subtly exposes the changing character of contemporary capitalism by inspecting how employers, unscrupulous agencies and landlords compete to drain dignity from the lives of our fellow citizens. Bloodworth reminds us that work is a contested, *deeply political* subject. But why should we need reminding of such an obvious point?

The simple answer is that work has been decoupled from politics. Much literature on work sidesteps political questions regarding the deployment of labour.[7] Over recent years the type of the work we do and why we do it have come to be understood as personal choices, a trade-off between work and leisure, rather than political ones. We will discuss below how and why work has been stripped of its political significance and been replaced by a largely ahistorical technical discussion of labour market statistical outcomes. This process speaks to the dominance of liberal economics and the defeat and intellectual weakness of the left with its withdrawal from theoretical and political interrogation of the character of work within modern capitalism.

Recent renewed interest in the organization of work and automation on the left has sought to correct this and once again politicize work. The danger is that this analysis misdiagnoses the problem and in doing so offers misguided remedies. We will argue that those on today's radical left who celebrate the 'end of work' and demand full automation help ensure that what was once a contested political terrain is vacated. There is even a tendency to identify this as a sign of political maturity and creativity rather than reflecting political defeat and neglect, indeed abandonment, of those the left historically sought to represent. At the sharp end, people can sense this betrayal; it helps account for fracturing political alliances and our electoral decline.

Bloodworth lives amongst those he observes. He provides not just a corrective to how we understand work, but also practical political voice to these workers. He has managed to capture a modern, often ignored, sense of grievance and humiliation conditioned by the changing work people do and the lives they live, compared to the ones they aspire to, indeed were promised, by generations of politicians. Such insights help us understand the political world we inhabit.

Hired explores how challenging employment and living conditions shape people's perceptions of their personal relationships as well as their bodies, diets and other people – chief amongst them politicians and immigrants. This coheres into a quiet anguish that resides within parts of the country. It is here that Bloodworth speaks to a deepening sense of national decay; one expressed in day-to-day frustrations with conventional politics. How we have got to this place goes beyond intellectual oversight; it reflects a wider failure to appreciate and understand the feelings experienced by our fellow citizens – a loss of empathy.

The feelings that Bloodworth explores are not simply derived from work itself, as meaningful work can offer a sense of status, solidarity and identity. The problem he pinpoints is the modern degradation of work and how this violates questions of human dignity. Yet we crowd these realities out of politics and policy and substitute concern with labour market aggregates. Consequently, the changing character of modern work remains under-researched and the deployment of labour considered beyond ethical and political contest.[8]

This was not always the case. Historically, the forms by which labour was understood as an economic and political category, together with how it was deployed, regulated and represented, underpinned alternative approaches to how society should itself be organized – competing theories of justice – and dominated politics. In the past the study of labour was fundamental to both political philosophy and the day-to-day practice of politics. Yet in recent years, especially on the left, we have withdrawn from these political traditions. It is a withdrawal that has come at great cost, for it has truncated our moral critique of capitalism and hedged our anger at the degraded work our fellow citizens are forced to perform. It has diminished the left and helps account for our insignificance.

These shifting intellectual loyalties tell a story whereby modern politics overturned the priorities of much radical thought of the nineteenth and twentieth centuries and its concern for human dignity. Today we suffer the collateral intellectual, cultural and political damage; we are losing our capacity to diagnose and resist the modern exploitation of our human capacity to work. We have neglected the significant role this capacity plays both in our personal lives and for capitalism more generally. This insight has been critical in the history of political economy and should once again inform our understanding of the world of work and capitalism. We will attempt to rehabilitate alternative approaches to human labour within the history of the left which have been lost. Those that pay the heaviest price for this intellectual neglect are those most degraded by modern work, vividly exposed by the effects of a small Covid-19 virus. The task is to re-establish a political method for the contemporary left to think once more about human labour.

Today capitalism appears unable to secure the material wellbeing of a critical mass of its citizens; it barely sustains itself. Even before a global pandemic triggered an economic earthquake, it was leading to what Pankaj Mishra described as 'mass disillusion, anger and disorientation caused by an increasingly unequal and unstable economy'.[9] This failure to deliver has implications for the ordering of society and how we thrive and live together; it is undermining the resilience of liberal democracy. We will argue the moral significance of work is critical in understanding these changes.

Authoritarian Populism

Democracy is endangered. Most obviously in countries like Russia, Turkey, Brazil, Poland and Hungary, but also in places with more resilient historical traditions, such as Italy and the United States. Here in the UK it is being severely tested. Having analysed global datasets covering 4 million people in 3,500 surveys across 154 countries, researchers recently concluded that dissatisfaction with democracy amongst the developed countries is at its highest levels for almost 25 years, and suggested the rise of populism was not so much a cause but symptom of this dissatisfaction. In the UK in 2019 dissatisfaction levels were the highest ever recorded. Another recent study of long-term shifts in public attitudes suggested growing UK disenchantment, declining confidence in parliamentary traditions and a willingness to embrace authoritarian ideas that 'challenge core tenets of our democracy'.[10] History has not ended, it has been upended. Modern liberal democracy, the political philosophy that told us competition was the guiding principle of human activity and the guarantor of true liberty, has incubated sinister new forms of populism.

Harvard professor Michael Sandel has argued that the

rise of authoritarian populism is best understood as the fault of the progressive left.[11] He suggests an 'economy of outrage' when reacting to the collection of right-wing populists gaining ground across the West, so that energy is channelled into creative intellectual and political responses. These would move beyond understandable protest and resistance, and address, dissect and remedy the fundamental failure of progressive politics, primarily its ethical detachment.

The hallmark of post-war social democracy was a moral desire to confront capital through the creation of the welfare state and wider strategies to contain and regulate the market. Yet the project became stale. Its concerns contracted towards the technocratic, often ineffective, administration of growth. The ethical energy of social democracy evaporated and was, by the late 1970s, effectively challenged by a resurgent New Right. The centre left politicians that succeeded Thatcher and Reagan, such as Blair, Clinton and Schröder, left unchallenged the essential market orthodoxies that preceded them. In office Obama succumbed to the same forces in contrast to the early moral clarity he expressed when running as insurgent candidate. Today's populist uprisings reflect a backlash against this soulless managerialism and offer an 'angry verdict' on a long-term liberal compact with capital; one that has entrenched economic and democratic inequalities and rolled back genuine social mobility. Any account of modern populism must recognize social democracy's loss of soul.

It is a powerful argument with challenging consequences. Rethinking the purpose of progressive politics requires moving beyond acknowledging economic grievance and enduring inequality. It requires a very different conversation, one that addresses *moral and cultural questions regarding the lives we wish to live,* and how the current disparity between that ideal and reality can find painful, often angry political expression driven by resentment and humiliation. Sandel locates in a global context the juxtaposition, or paradox, of personal hope and practical despair that Bloodworth identified regarding the work we wish for compared to what we perform.

Sandel suggests the left requires a new telos, a new public philosophy, in order to respond to this epic challenge. To help this reformation, he identifies four themes for progressive politics to confront, linked to questions of work, human labour and the creation of community.

First is the need for economic strategy to engineer inclusive growth, one that confronts the escalating inequality which feeds today's authoritarian impulses. Such redesign must rethink wealth creation and distribution, including that created by and apportioned to human labour.

His second suggestion involves the language used by today's liberal progressives, emphasizing opportunity and the removal of barriers to success. Meritocracy, a term initially coined in the UK as an ironic description to justify inaction over inequality, has further entrenched elite privilege. Sandel urges us to challenge the harsh judgements that liberals and progressives impose on those who are viewed as 'unsuccessful' in a meritocracy – not least in the resentment this builds, fuelling backlash. It adds to a sense of cultural detachment in politics and a disrespect for the work performed by many of our fellow citizens. Having valorized financial and educational achievement, we appear ill-equipped to understand the feelings of those that live outside these defined parameters of success. This needs to change, as today's progressives are developing a politics tacitly aimed at, and embraced by, society's winners.

The third theme relates to the meaning and future of work and how this will affect the lives we wish to lead. Our economies have been reoriented away from building things to managing money. Material reward and social esteem have closely followed, drifting away from the traditional jobs carried out by the working class whose prospects look increasingly endangered. We are told that technological change might further erode the dignity of such work or render it obsolete. Many on the progressive left have embraced such thinking.

For instance, for Tony Blair and New Labour, knowledge work signalled the end of the post-war economy and traditional Labour approaches to work. The working class was on the wrong side of history. Knowledge work was the future, and the famous meritocratic slogan 'education, education, education' captured an economic policy focused on human capital. This false technological nirvana is resurrected today by utopian 'post-work' theorists who embrace Universal Basic Income (UBI) to take us there. Such an approach can suggest a certain disdain for jobs not considered worthwhile, reinforce the detachment of progressive thinking and help build the forces driving authoritarian populism. Whether we wish to welcome or resist such a future in the years ahead, the nature and future of work will be critical themes for progressive politics in any new telos.

Finally, Sandel requests renewed concern for the moral significance of national boundaries, a philosophical request for politics to return to its classical origins in terms of the creation of community. The rise of the populist right is inseparable from the politics of community and nation – unfashionable terrain for the left.

In order to rebuild the ethical character of the left, therefore, it must accept its own culpability in any account of our unstable democracies. This will not be easy. It requires a politics of work, something we have lost. Moreover, modern progressive thinking has tended to embrace a liberal cosmopolitanism in ways that assert a privileged global citizenship over other forms of fidelity and attachment. Sandel suggests a set of moral obligations to specific electorates whereby politicians seek to build resilient, stable communities – ones that share sacrifice, risk and reward within defined boundaries.

Overall, to challenge the modern story of dispossession and abandonment offered by the populist right, progressives must forge a positive reimagination of community and nation anchored within a politics of work. This will not be straightforward because it returns to the contested terrain of belonging, community and nation where many immediately detect reactionary, exclusive associations.

The Challenge

It is often remarked that we are living through a crisis of neo-liberalism, a specific approach to the market, economy and society that captured politics; a doctrine now exposed as unable to deliver what it promised. The resulting discontent has sought to reconfigure domestic politics and found expression in Brexit. The three creeds that dominated the last century, conservatism, liberalism and social democracy, encased within our Tory, Liberal and Labour traditions, are all threatened by their embrace of the market through the neo-liberal turn. Each now seeks reinvention with mixed success.

Conservatism capitulated to the economic liberals. Fundamental beliefs, such as order, freedom and the pres- ervation of our national institutions, were compromised as a fringe thought experiment took over and derailed a once great political party. This has inhibited its ability to widen opportunity through a property-owning democracy and forge inclusive growth protected by sound money. In response, and having secured Brexit, Boris Johnson and his top team now seek a 'blue-collar' conservatism and spend- ing plan to appeal to its new 'Red Wall' constituencies. Their future success post-pandemic will depend on how far the party and wider conservative intellectual movement remain attached to the economic arguments of the liberal purists.

Social democracy remains a stale project barely recog- nizable when compared to the post-war movement to civilize capitalism. Thatcher's legacy hung over the 'Third Way' project to manage the proceeds of growth; it won three elections but was swept out of office without growth to manage. Corbyn broke with the 'Third Way' and delivered a 10-point jump in support at the 2017 election. 'Corbynism' had energy because it stood outside the neo-liberal appropriation of UK politics; yet much of the party did not. The party was battered in 2019 and under new leadership remains a brittle, nervous coalition.

Within the Liberal Democrats the centre-left social liberal tradition lost out to the 'Orange Book' economic hardliners. This takeover secured a move into coalition government, but with a significant price attached on becoming the fall guys for the 2017 election defeat.

These tensions predate the shake down of a global pandemic. All three traditions appear ill-equipped to offer post-pandemic renewal. Something new is desperately needed as epic economic contraction will likely see austerity and neo-liberalism re-emerge despite having endangered liberal democracy since the financial crisis. In 2007–8, after the bankers broke the financial system, politicians absolved the finance sector with little penance and imposed austerity on the backs of the poor. The public rightly identified the bailout as breaching the laws of natural justice, especially when forced to pay for it in shrinking incomes and service cuts. Such immorality inspired populist revolt, yet the cycle is in danger of being repeated. With such limited intellectual resources to draw on, we are in danger of repeating history with disastrous implications for how we live together. Renewed austerity looks economically inevitable and yet politically impossible.

Sandel's four building blocks can help shape a radical rethink. His argument is subtle and asks philosophical questions we cannot indefinitely avoid. On the one hand, progressives have been too concerned with allocating resources; technocratic and limited in their appreciation of the lives people wish to live which stretch beyond material concerns. On the other, we recoil from moral questions because of our insistence on liberal neutrality. In doing so, we disengage from the fundamental issues that feed the populist right: questions of worth, esteem, resentment and humiliation. We inhabit a world detached from the people, in our language of rights, opportunity and fairness that 'flattens questions of meaning, identity and purpose'.

This is all quietly devastating. It helps account for the populist right by diagnosing how social democracy succumbed to the drumbeat of neo-liberalism. Yet it is not just that we handed ethical questions to the market. It is the way, even today, our continued belief in liberal procedural justice has removed moral questions from public discussion and allowed authoritarian voices to monopolize this terrain. Sandel echoes, on a larger canvass, the day-to-day concerns revealed by Bloodworth. The challenge is to align the insights of both writers to rebuild a politics of work, part of a wider public philosophy to combat the insurgent populist right.

The End of Work?

Before the pandemic took grip, the future world of work was attracting widespread attention. It was regularly discussed within popular culture, modern literature, journalism and social, economic and political commentary; it had become part of the everyday conversation. Two poles emerged in the general debate. One signposts a post-work nightmare of escalating inequality amongst a threatened humanity subservient to technology, the other a future utopia of abundance, numerous routes to self-actualization and even enhanced transhuman possibilities, with lots in between.

This renewed interest in work futures, existing before a global health crisis derailed the economy, reflects a widespread belief that 'the robots are coming'. A few key texts have been highly significant in shaping this narrative of epic transformation, indeed revolution. MIT's Andrew McAfee and Erik Brynjolfsson have suggested automation and AI are powering a new 'second machine age', equivalent to the first Industrial Revolution, one that will further exacerbate inequality.[12] Another popular contribution, by Martin Ford,[13] has confirmed these technological shifts yet imagines a more optimistic future if humanity can leverage these changes to save a burning planet and resolve structural unemployment. Such books shape a narrative depicting a world on the edge of epochal technological change. It is also often described as the 'fourth industrial revolution', one which will redraw how we live, in ways we cannot even imagine. The first revolution refers to the way steam and water powered and mechanized production. The second highlights the effects of electrification while the third signals transformations by information technology. The fourth identifies the upheaval brought on by digital technologies – among them AI, augmented reality, 3-D printing – transforming all sections of society, politics, communities, our relations and who we are as humans.

The discussion triggers numerous tabloid headlines when this general change story translates into a concrete numbers game of displaced jobs through automation. Many of the most threatening estimates of technological unemployment can be traced to a single source, a 2013 article by Carl Frey and Mike Osborne, which suggested nearly half of the types of jobs used by the US Bureau of Labor remain vulnerable to automation.[14] This has been regularly used to suggest the demise of many millions of traditional blue-collar jobs. Almost as a companion piece, in *The Future of the Professions* Richard and Daniel Susskind suggest technological forces will dramatically rework white-collar professional jobs such as lawyers, consultants, accountants and health professionals.[15] The cumulative effect implies no one is safe from technological upheaval and the inevitable end of work. This also has major geopolitical implications, a 'great displacement', with unemployment unevenly distributed within and between countries.[16]

Against this backdrop of uncharted technological disruption and the destruction of work, infinite space is created for all sorts of writers to insert themselves into the story and interpret our future. In some versions people appear as victims in foreseen dystopias; in others human values shape the forces of production to benefit humanity and the planet. Writers pick and mix from the available data to validate a personal or political worldview. Assorted novelists, commentators and politicians selectively mould the material into a speculative literature prone to overassertion. Yet it has established a noise of rupture, one that allows writers to dramatize the human dilemmas posed by AI and our liberation from routine, dehumanized work. In Ian McEwan's recent book, for instance, technological breakthroughs allow the writer to contemplate love and humanity and the ethical challenges posed by cyborg augmentation.[17]

The depiction of alternative worlds through epochal technological change is a site where fiction and politics have met regularly. Critically, however, modern utopian thinking on the left tends to invert the political usage of science fiction in the hands of writers such as Wells and Orwell. Throughout the early twentieth century, science fiction allowed parts of the left to reassert the need for human solidarity and political agency to contest the malign consequences of our intellectual development. Science fiction retained an ethical, humanist character. Left unchallenged, technological change could usher in tyranny; the human imperative was to ensure this was not left unchallenged. Even those texts that appear dystopian – such as Huxley's *Brave New World* or Orwell's *Nineteen Eighty-Four* – were political interventions; warning shots to choke off dystopian trends in modern society.[18] Huxley's target was the dominant left utilitarianism, Orwell the totalitarian, scientific left. Sadly, it is a different story today. In the last century, writers used science fiction to warn humanity, now commentators such as Aaron Bastani and Ash Sakar use technological disruption to foresee 'communist utopia'.[19]

Tech-utopianism has become a defining characteristic on the modern left, possibly as a safe space to inoculate against the daily grind of electoral defeat – a political Hail Mary against loss and decay. In a tragic rerun it echoes the technological determinism of generations of Marxists. History repeats and is captured in influential articles and books discussing 'accelerationism' and 'fully automated luxury communism' and is perhaps best represented in Paul Mason's innovative and hugely popular book *PostCapitalism*.[20]

The political embrace of automation also corresponds with renewed interest in the idea of UBI, to rid us from what the late anthropologist David Graeber considered the modern indignity of degraded, meaningless work and 'bullshit jobs'.[21] UBI has become the signature policy for automated new times. The idea of a minimum income first appeared at the beginning of the sixteenth century, and of an unconditional one-off grant at the end of the eighteenth century. The two combined to form an unconditional basic income near the middle of the nineteenth century. Fashionable debate concerning technological change, structural unemployment and the rise of the robots has brought UBI to a bigger audience.

The idea has widespread political support. The traditional right-wing case stretches back centuries and predates our modern safety nets. More recent advocates, such as Milton Friedman, Friedrich Hayek, Charles Murray and Richard Nixon have embraced it as a vehicle to roll back the welfare state and replace it with an individualized transaction between the state and the consumer. The traditional left-wing case has tended to focus on the basic human right to a level of subsistence, not just to survive but to guarantee freedom. An unconditional, universal safety net is said to be essential to shield against work poverty or job loss and build the power of labour relative to capital. A 'proto-UBI' was advocated by Tom Paine, and more recent supporters include Bertrand Russell, J.K. Galbraith and Lyndon Johnson. It is a policy embraced by many Silicon Valley titans, possibly to offset their personal responsibilities for structural unemployment, as well as technology writers such as Martin Ford and presidential nominee Andrew Yang.

Support for UBI in anticipation of rampant technological unemployment has led to an upsurge of interest in recent basic income initiatives. These include the late 1970s Manitoba Mincome annual income project and the Alaskan oil dividend as well as modern UBI pilots in Finland, Scotland, Canada, Oakland, the Netherlands and New Zealand. Debate about the merits of UBI compared to job generation programmes is underway. In the United States, progressive democrats such as Kirsten Gillibrand, Cory Booker and Bernie Sanders are part of a growing movement to embrace the idea of a federal job guarantee. The government would guarantee a well-paying job, with benefits and salary to establish a new subsistence threshold to cover housing, food, childcare, health insurance and pension arrangements like New Deal employment programmes. Yet both Barack Obama and Hillary Clinton appear more attracted to the idea of UBI. Here in the UK, John McDonnell has argued the case for UBI, as has the centre left organization Compass and the writer Guy Standing.[22]

Pragmatic Confusion

Whilst the march of the machines has renewed interest in work, so too have more pragmatic political concerns about insecure jobs and our enduring economic weaknesses. Famously, outside 10 Downing Street on 13 July 2016, on becoming prime minister Theresa May talked of 'fighting against the burning injustices ... If you're from an ordinary working-class family, life is much harder than many people in Westminster realize. You have a job, but you don't always have job security ... The government I lead will be driven not by the interests of the privileged few, but by yours.'

This was widely recognized as a significant shift, at least

rhetorically, towards 'blue-collar' conservatism with a focus on 'ordinary working people' reflecting the influence of 'Red Tory' or 'post-liberal' elements at the top of the party. It suggested a reorientation away from labour market deregulation of the Thatcher era and a renewed interest in work quality. In October 2016, May commissioned Matthew Taylor to report on how employment practices could change to keep pace with modern business models.[23]

The 2017 Conservative Election Manifesto announced: 'we do not believe in untrammelled free markets' and 'we reject the cult of selfish individualism. We abhor social division, injustice, unfairness and inequality' and suggested an overhaul of labour market policy and embrace of industrial democracy by putting workers on the boards. On 11 July 2017, Taylor's review was unveiled and drew a scathing response from across the trade union movement. Since publication, there has been little evidence of actual policy follow-through.

This shift wasn't really about policy. In the aftermath of the Brexit referendum, the Conservative Party were seeking to focus on workplace issues given the shifting class alignments amongst the electorate. Driven by the European question, the party was on walkabout in search of a policy agenda to consolidate working-class support, a move that foreshadowed their 2019 election victory in 'Red Wall' seats and appeals to 'Workington Man'.

Renewed political interest for workplace issues also aligned with expert policy concerns with the UK productivity 'puzzle' – the appalling domestic productivity performance since the 2008 financial crash. What is striking is the contrast between the noise of rupture – the language of epochal technological change and end of work – alongside record jobs levels and 'puzzling' productivity numbers. Sometime soon we might expect the structural unemployment to show up or the productive lift derived by automation to arrive.

Without doubt UK productivity continues to underperform in terms of long-term domestic trends and compared to other major economies. It also underperforms compared to what followed the two previous major recessions of 1979–80 and 1990–1. There are no agreed answers as to why. Is it the product of an enduring economic shock, or changing patterns of labour, or simply a lack of demand?[24]

The Bank of England cannot account for this 'puzzle'. The then governor comically stated in 2015, 'It has been worse than we had expected and worse than we had expected for the last several years. We have been successively disappointed'.

Then Worked Stopped

Then our lives were threatened, and work stopped. In the US, 20 million jobs were lost in April 2020 alone, 8.6 million in leisure and hospitality. In the UK for the same month the ONS calculated an unemployment rise of 856,000 to 2.1 million, the biggest monthly increase since modern records began. On 15 April, the Universal Credit director general briefed that 1.4 million people had signed up for Universal Credit in the preceding four weeks. That same month the number of people on PAYE fell by 457,000. The immediate economic outlook would have been much bleaker if not for the government's furlough scheme, the biggest labour market intervention in history. Many companies did not lay off staff straight away because for six months the Treasury picked up the tab for 80 per cent of monthly pay up to a limit of £2,500. Yet this package suspended rather than resolved the employment effects of the virus. Without the wage subsidies covering 8 million jobs, the UK would have faced an unemployment rate approaching 20 per cent in early 2020. Yet the country continues to face an epic work challenge.

Some sectors were disproportionately affected immediately by the pandemic; the accommodation and food services sector, the arts, entertainment and recreation sectors had the largest number of firms decreasing staff working hours. Around 15 per cent of employees were working in a sector that was immediately, largely or entirely shut down during the initial period of lockdown. From the outset the virus proved to be unequal. Some workers were disproportionally impacted. Low-paid workers were more likely to work in shut-down sectors and less likely to be able to work from home, as were the young. One-third of employees in the bottom 10 per cent of earners worked in shut-down sectors, and less than 10 per cent of the bottom half of earners could work from home.

The pandemic and the prospect of death forced us to reassess what we value in our own lives and the lives of others. We applauded health and care workers. We re-evaluated the work of hairdressers, delivery drivers and a range of public servants, social workers, supermarket operatives and an array of tradespeople. We were forced to rethink how we value and reward the contribution of millions of front-line workers. Will the economy that emerges after the pandemic honour and respect the dignity of this work?

The Way Ahead

The following pages weave together these theoretical and practical topics by rethinking work. We will rehabilitate certain intellectual and political traditions in the understanding of human labour and the regulation of employment and in so doing criticize a lot of fashionable thinking. The book is divided into two parts. The first discusses the economics of labour and demarcates post-war politics in terms of competing narratives regarding employment regulation; the second looks at labour from an ethical orientation referenced through competing theories of justice.

We begin in chapter 2 with the post-war industrial relations diagnosis of the so-called 'British disease', the rise of the corporatist state and pluralist attempts to embed the organized working class into a regulated polity and economy. Such an approach echoed earlier concerns with the division of labour and the distribution of just rewards contained within nineteenth-century Classical Political Economy.

In chapter 3 we look at the emergence of the British New Right and the Thatcherite supply-side revolution, which its advocates asserted had achieved by the early 1990s a UK productivity 'miracle'. We study the way the right sought to politically operationalize Neo-Classical Economics. We discuss how assumptions of predetermined human labour and the rational personal trade-off between work and leisure succeeded in decoupling work and politics.

Chapter 4 looks at labour regulation under New Labour, the effects of the 2008 economic crash and our bewildering modern productivity 'puzzle'. We inspect how competing approaches to labour regulation sought influence after 1997 and how Blair eventually succumbed to a form of technological determinism that continues to blight the modern left.

We complete Part I by engaging with modern-day arguments regarding postcapitalism and utopian assumptions of a workless future. This in-vogue literature inherits a deterministic reading of value theory and misunderstands Marx's approach to human labour under capitalism with damaging political consequences for the left today, at times cruelly exposed in 'Corbynism'.

This journey through post-war history suggests we urgently need to develop new ways of thinking about human labour. In Part II we attempt to provide such an alternative by discussing justice and human labour. We begin in chapter 6 by inspecting the nature of work and its history. We use this to develop our understanding of the dignity of labour. Chapter 7 is concerned with our personal feelings regarding the labour we perform. We review what we know about what work can offer in terms of personal status, security and identity. Finally, we inspect what we know and what we don't about the future of work and competing assumptions regarding the future demand for labour.

In chapter 8 we attempt to rehabilitate an approach to human labour excluded from modern social democratic and socialist thinking. We contrast this approach to justice, excised from today's progressive conversation, with more popular deterministic and utilitarian thinking on the left. The concluding chapter 9 returns to the crises of liberal democracy and the rise of authoritarian populism. We discuss modern politics and post-pandemic labour regulation and end with an inspection of UBI and some practical suggestions for the organization and regulation of labour.

The basic argument is a simple one: the dignity of labour should inform how we order society and contribute to the renewal of a social democratic vision of justice.

Part I: The Economics of Labour

Work and human labour are clutch political issues.

In this first part of the book we chronologically address the political representation of labour since the end of the Second World War and inspect how various economic frameworks have directed alternative approaches to labour regulation.

Throughout we reflect on the influence of Classical Political Economy, Marxism and Neo-Classical Economics in shaping competing political debates on labour regulation. The first considers embodied labour as the source of a commodity's value, the second the exploitation of a person's capacity to work as the source of profit under capitalism, whilst the third essentially ignores the organization of work. Each abstract economic framework has influenced the study of industrial relations, industrial sociology and personnel management, and we review their contributions in post-war debates over the organization of work.

The story shifts from post-war social democracy by way of Thatcherism to fractured neo-liberalism and fashionable Marxism and ends in modern political bewilderment and a desperate desire for something different; a journey navigated through the contested political representation of human labour.

2
The Labour Problem

Dagenham and the 17

The labour problem in the decades after the war was the Dagenham story. Early skilled unions had fought to protect their jobs through controlled access to their trades. Later, in contrast, the industrial organization of the unskilled and semi-skilled was built around numerical power, reflected in the emergence of general unions. During the 1950s and 1960s, these unions expanded in the car plants and battled to control the labour process. This Dagenham story was a world away from the nostalgia of *Made in Dagenham*.[1]

During the 1950s and 1960s the idea of the agitator regularly appeared in films like the BAFTA-winning *The Angry Silence* and *I'm All Right Jack*. In the former drama, factory worker Richard Attenborough stands alone against intimidation in his refusal to take part in unofficial action orchestrated by the militant steward played by Bernard Lee. In the latter satire, released a year earlier in 1959, Peter Sellers played militant missile factory steward Fred Kite whose actions in opposition to a 'time and motion man' and incompetent management eventually bring the country to a standstill.

On the Dagenham estate by the mid-1950s, the technical capacity of management to 'speed up' the line had been enhanced following years of heavy investment. A million and a half vehicles were built as the struggle to control line speed and contest local management prerogative intensified. Unique for the automotive sector, Ford refused payment through piece rates or plant bargaining over workloads. This guaranteed shop floor militancy and ongoing confrontation.

Immediately after the end of the Second World War, Ford reluctantly recognized Dagenham shop stewards after 11,000 workers downed tools and stopped production. Yet the company refused to concede any power in the plants and would only negotiate with full-time union officials in central London through the National Joint Negotiating Committee (NJNC). In 1955, twenty-two unions signed a formal national procedure to centralize negotiations within the company. Decades of suspicion followed between Dagenham workers, the local stewards and union full-time officials negotiating on their behalf.

In March 1953, Ford took over the Briggs Motor Bodies plant. Briggs had followed the company from Detroit in 1932 to manufacture sheet steel, bodies and stampings and was located at Dagenham Dock next to the assembly sites. Briggs experienced intense workplace battles throughout the 1930s and by the early 1940s had strong shop floor organization. Unlike Ford, they had conceded plant bargaining and piece rates. Once the plant had been acquired by Ford, these practices were ruthlessly whittled away, resulting in hundreds of unofficial disputes, stoppages and sackings to preserve management control across the estate.

By 1960, the *Voice of Ford Workers* – the paper of the Dagenham Joint Shop Stewards – was selling 50,000 copies weekly; it had become the strongest, richest unofficial union organization in the country. The tension between local activist power and a company intent on rejecting plant bargaining played out over battles to 'speed up' the line. In the Paint Trim and Assembly plant (the PTA) alone some 400,000 hours were lost through strikes in 1962.

The crunch occurred after the PTA walked out after the sacking of a popular steward, Bill Francis. The company selectively re-employed all those left outside the gates apart from seventeen, a group containing a key cadre of communist stewards. A public court of enquiry – with head office union representation – upheld the sackings in one of the signature battles in post-war British labour relations. The power of the independent shop stewards and unofficial Dagenham unionism was broken by a management driven from Michigan with tacit support within the formal union machinery; a defeat whose repercussions played out over decades and are still remembered locally even today. For many, the Dagenham story symbolized the post-war 'British disease' and the social democratic response was industrial pluralism.

Post-war Pluralism

Pluralist labour relations traditions stress the inevitability of workplace conflict given the plurality of interests within complex social systems such as Ford. Such interest groups, including management and workers, represent conflicting sites of authority over the organization and regulation of employment. The management of such conflict is key to both the success of the enterprise and the wider economy. Emphasis is placed on methods to efficiently represent these legitimate, competing interests. Unions and collective bargaining express the collective voice of the workers and can serve to regulate conflict and counteract the unilateral, over-mighty rule of the employer and achieve just outcomes. John Dunlop's 1958 approach to industrial relations through Systems Theory stands as a landmark pluralist approach.[2]

Its clearest, most comprehensive expression can be found

with the so-called 'Oxford', later 'Warwick', tradition of
industrial relations analysis, especially in the work of Allan
Flanders and Hugh Clegg.[3] This understanding of what in
the nineteenth century was labelled 'the labour problem'
influenced government policy for decades and remains
a vital, albeit neglected, contribution in the evolution of
post-war social democracy. This school attempted to build
institutions to moderate and reconcile power relations at
work in order to address the widespread post-war industrial unrest that broke out in communities like Dagenham
to help secure a shared national prosperity. They upheld
an approach to human labour widely shared a century
before.

Classical Economics and the Labour Problem

Twentieth-century politics has been foreshadowed by the
way late nineteenth-century economists reorientated their
discipline into a formulation of prices and away from
questions of human labour. It was no accident. The distribution of commodities and wealth was from then on to be
understood as the efficient market realization of individual
subjective preferences, the cornerstone of liberal economics and what we call 'neo-liberalism'.

Classical Political Economy (CPE), on the other hand,
with its origins in eighteenth-century Enlightenment,
offered a very different understanding of the distribution
of economic resources. This body of work interpreted the
stages of human history through the study of alternative
modes of subsistence, principally hunting and gathering,
pastoralism, agrarian society and commercial relations.
It was primarily associated with Adam Smith and David
Ricardo but includes other writers such as J.S. Mill and
Thomas Malthus.[4]

CPE is basically a theory of production, or specifically
a theory of expanded production, upon which distribution and exchange relations are understood. It offered a

distributional politics of class reconciliation through management of the outcome of this growth. For both Ricardo and Smith, the three classes of landlords, workers and capitalists were identified in accordance with the distribution of revenues associated with the three factors of production – land, labour and capital – the so-called 'Trinity Formula'.

For Adam Smith the extension of commerce through free trade offered the opportunity to build an independent economy and open civil society to enhance liberty and crowd out tyranny. Modern growth, expanding productive capacity with the division of labour, meant value was created independent of land prices or by the hoarding of scarce resources and offered the prospect of enhanced wealth and class reconciliation. Given the significance of the division of labour in expanding productivity, human labour was for Smith the measure of the value of the commodities produced. He maintained a theory of economic and social progress built around free trade and a theory of value grounded in the labour times embodied in commodities.[5]

David Ricardo shared this basic insight of a labour theory of value.[6] He sought to understand class relations through the form by which human labour defines the price of commodities. Specifically, he sought to scientifically establish that the amount of labour necessary to produce commodities determined their price; in effect that price and value were the same.

Both Smith and Ricardo analysed income distribution between classes through studying relations within production. Economic expansion alongside institutional arrangements such as enhanced education provision could help advance all the social classes. This link between class reconciliation through economic growth and institutional maturity is a recurring theme in the history of social democracy and informs long-established traditions on the left today, including Fabianism. The problem occurs when there is no growth to manage and redistribute. A much earlier inability to engineer growth stimulated working-class organization and political uncertainty, which ultimately provoked a revolution in economic thinking in the 1870s.

This relationship between labour and value is a theme that will reappear throughout the rest of the book. A specific approach to value as one physically embodied in commodities by concrete labour has informed various traditions on the left which tend to promote an essentially utilitarian distributional politics. This is most clearly expressed in a traditional pluralist focus on the distribution of the proceeds of growth to enable political reconciliation. However, as we shall see, it is also the hallmark of more radical contemporary analysis of automation which envisions immanent crises enveloping capitalism because of the declining proportion of physical labour invested in commodities. Within this modern literature, not only is labour being displaced by technology but so too is capitalism itself. As the wage-labour relationship evaporates, then politics refracts onto wider distributional conflicts within society rather than class relations defined by the character of the employment relationship. We will describe this as 'Ricardian' in that these political concerns can theoretically be traced back to those of CPE, best captured in Ricardo's attempts to calculate price and value through embodied labour times.

These highly technical and at times mystifying assumptions regarding the relationship between value and labour have helped define the politics of the last few centuries although they are very rarely discussed. They will be recurring themes in the pages that follow as they have shaped fundamental political disagreements both within and between the left and right.

At this stage, however, we simply need to make the point that this search for an economic theory of value built around embodied labour contained unresolved tensions within CPE; tensions that again also reappear today. Smith's approach to the division of labour considers value through the actual embodied labour times in the goods produced, although confusingly at times also in terms of labour commanded – as the quantity of labour that *could* be employed. Ricardo was more precise in his theory of price or value driven by the amount of labour contained within the commodity. The problem for Ricardo and 'Ricardians' appears when prices and values diverge. As we shall see, this same problem also confronts writers such as Paul Mason on today's left who produce overconfident assertions of automation upending capitalism through displaced human labour. Their understanding of capitalist stability is hinged around a highly contentious assumption of embodied labour times as the source of value and therefore echoes Ricardo's historic method of price calculation. For these modern commentators, automation breaks the link between labour and value, triggering crisis and transition beyond capitalism, with such assumptions enabling them to loudly assert a series of highly contentious electoral strategies for the left.

However, notwithstanding certain ambiguities regarding profit, value and labour, the importance of CPE lay in approaching the value of commodities in terms of the labour times invested in them. It acknowledged the need for economics to understand how labour is organized, represented and regulated through study of the workplace. Work was inherently political because the income distribution between classes was dependent on the organization of production. These historic concerns of political economy reappeared in post-war pluralist industrial relations analysis to confront an emerging British sickness.

Disease

From once being characterized as the 'workshop of the world' in the later part of the nineteenth century, with its worldwide export of manufacturing commodities, Britain gradually declined as an industrial power in the post-war period. Productivity growth had begun to lag that in the United States before the Second World War. Comparative decline within Europe began in the 1950s during post-war economic reconstruction, becoming entrenched by the 1960s.

Politicians on the right began to argue that the UK's economic problems originated in the unique system of labour relations that had resulted from the speed and timing of British industrialization. Exceptional protections were available to unions as they remained immune from prosecution. Worker organizations were granted the freedom to strike and organize by being protected from civil damages following the 1906 Trade Disputes Act. As collective bodies, unions were shielded from tortious liability when they induced breaches of the employment contract. This helped establish the tradition of *voluntarism* as the hallmark of British labour law. In effect the law was kept out of regulating employment relations in favour of a more laissez-faire approach. Negative legal immunities from prosecution were preferred over individual and collective legal rights. Arguably, the British Labour Party was created to retain this separation between labour relations and the law, following the famous Taff Vale judgment which had imperilled both the right to strike and the future viability of the union movement.

This voluntarist tradition was upheld by the Attlee Labour government, with labour market policy focused on overall levels of employment. The unions emerged out of the Second World War politically and industrially strengthened. Bevin at the Ministry of Labour had created scores of 'joint industrial councils' and new wages councils. By the 1950s strains were showing as low unemployment and labour shortages triggered strikes and inflation as workers gained greater power within the workplace. The narrative of the 'British disease' emerged, and with it the tag of 'the sick man of Europe', tying together these labour and productivity concerns. Voluntarism had created a fragmented industrial relations system which inhibited growth. Uncoordinated free collective bargaining – the British labour movement's preferred route to industrial democracy – lay at the heart of a problem which found expression in wage drift, inefficient, restricted work practices and unofficial action.

Conservative politicians began to target comparative systems of labour regulation in their search for answers to questions of global competitiveness.[7] In 1958, in *A Giant's Strength*, a group of conservative lawyers laid the blame at the system of labour law,[8] a theme later picked up in July 1961 by Harold Macmillan in the first early attempts to introduce a pay norm and debates influencing the creation of the National Economic Development Council (NEDC) in 1962. Later, the incoming Wilson government felt it necessary to confront the question of labour reform by drawing on the diagnosis of a group of industrial relations academics in the consolidation of British corporatism. This approach sought to establish a tripartite union-employer-state architecture to integrate the organized working class into a national project to boost competitiveness and anchor post-war social democracy.

The Cure

Over fifty years ago, *New Society* first identified the new Oxford School as central to British post-war reconstruction.[9] Their contribution has been neglected in the study of post-war politics and deserves a rehabilitation.[10] For decades this group influenced the development of government thinking on economic and industrial strategy, pay policy, employment law, trade union reform, economic democracy and much more. The central task, as they saw it, was to build institutions to moderate unequal power relations at work – to civilize capitalism.

The Oxford School sought a post-war pluralist settlement to regulate capital, a nation-specific corporatism, through the extension of collective bargaining. Many of its key figures had direct personal wartime experiences of fascism, communism and later German reconstruction, which influenced their approach to the evolution of post-war social democracy. The tradition endured and informed labour regulation debates throughout the post-war years even up to the early New Labour period, especially with George Bain and Willy Brown at the Low Pay Commission, John Monks at the TUC and Ian McCartney as employment minister. As early as the late 1940s, Flanders described his approach as the 'third way', a phrase given greater prominence in the 1990s by Tony Blair and Tony Giddens.

These academics sought to humanize work, not through abstract theory, textbook modelling or economic algebra, but following extensive research into the practical realities of the world of work – literally the day-to-day study of the workplace and how human labour was deployed and regulated. Unlike today, systematic practical research into the workplace informed public policy, an approach culminating in the Donovan Report.

The Royal Commission on Trade Unions and Employers' Associations, with Lord Donovan as chair, was established in April 1965 and its final report was published in 1968. It was a direct response to mounting evidence of comparative industrial decline and escalating productivity shortfalls and the clearest expression of post-war industrial pluralism with the following remit:

> to consider relations between managements and employees and the role of trade unions and employers' associations in promoting the interests of their members and in accelerating the social and economic advance of the nation, with particular reference to the law affecting the activities of these bodies, and report.

The report[11] upheld the voluntarist traditions of UK labour law – of legal abstention and collective laissez faire. Instead of overhauling the system of labour legislation, the preferred solution was the reform and extension of collective bargaining and the protection of the rights of individual employees and union members. It believed:

Properly conducted, collective bargaining is the most effective means of giving workers the right to representation in decisions affecting their working lives, a right which is or should be the prerogative of every worker in a democratic society.

Yet it also criticized Britain's traditional bargaining and 'the disorder in factory and workshop relations and pay structures promoted by the conflict between the formal and informal system'. The formal system was embodied in the official institutions of industry-wide collective bargaining to regulate the conditions of employment. The informal system comprised the relationships which had developed in individual establishments at various levels: between trade unions and employer and between managers, shop stewards and workers.

Nowhere was Donovan's diagnosis of tension between these two systems more clearly on display than in the Dagenham plants. It reflected the tense, uneasy relations between a powerful, autonomous shop steward network and the formal hierarchies of both union and NJNC negotiating bodies, played out in relentless conflicts to control the production line.

The Corporate State

The Donovan Report suggested the solution to these industrial showdowns lay in reconciling competing systems of labour regulation. It identified a pathway out of comparative decline, to resolve earnings drift and unofficial strikes through innovative factory agreements to boost productivity and formalize labour relations.[12]

The report proposed an Industrial Relations Act to register collective agreements, extend collective bargaining and remove barriers to union recognition. It tasked the Industrial Relations Commission to investigate anti-union discrimination, collective agreement registration issues and union recognition disputes, and to enquire into long-term industrial relations problems.

Union rules were to be considered by a Chief Registrar of Trade Unions and Employers Associations. It recommended an independent review body to adjudicate complaints by union members and legislation to safeguard employees against unfair dismissal.[13] These rights would apply from the first day of employment, without a qualifying period.[14] Industrial tribunals were to be renamed labour tribunals with an enlarged jurisdiction.

The strategy was to incorporate the working class into the governance of industry. Although such thinking pre-dated Donovan, the 1968 report stands as the hallmark of post-war Oxford pluralism. Such an approach influenced the creation of the NEDC in 1962 with its sectoral tripartite Economic Development Committees, 'Little Neddies', to reverse economic decline and the short-lived – pre-sterling crisis – National Plan of 1965, and later, the state merchant banks such as the National Enterprise Board (NEB) and the wider corporatist architecture – the Health and Safety Executive (HSE), the Manpower Services Commission (MSC), the Advisory, Conciliation and Arbitration Service (ACAS) and the National Board for Prices and Incomes. The strategy also sought to address wage drift and shop steward strength, not just with productivity bargaining but also tripartite attempts at wage norms, targets and a variety of incomes policies.

On publication, Donovan was largely welcomed by the TUC. Yet incomes policies, strike levels and trade union influence were hot political issues and the Labour leadership were subtly moving against the spirit of the Oxford School. By the late 1960s, the Wilson government was looking to tighten the regulation of labour. Ray Gunter had pressed hard against unofficial action when at the Ministry of Labour. The department was renamed the Department of Employment and Productivity under Barbara Castle and she too sought new legal remedies. Controversial legalistic attempts to confront shop steward power emerged with the 1969 White Paper *In Place of Strife* and later with Heath's 1971 Industrial Relations Act, new labour courts and codes to regulate industrial relations practices.

In Place of Strife, whilst accepting the overall Donovan diagnosis, also proposed a 28-day conciliation pause, new ballot regulations and powers to intervene in union recognition disputes. Such initiatives rested uncomfortably with the principles of voluntarism and, although subsequently abandoned, weakened Wilson's government before its eventual defeat in May 1970.

The 1970 Equal Pay Act – a direct response to the Dagenham seamstresses' strike – appeared more in keeping with the spirit of Donovan. However, on closer inspection it is difficult to decouple the walkout by these women machinists from the ongoing East London political battles that finally broke Labour's industrial relations reforms and signposted the turbulent politics of the 1970s.

Rethinking *Made in Dagenham*

In contrast to Nigel Cole's cosy 2010 story, the machinists' strike was part of the ongoing post-war battle to regulate labour within Ford and across the country at large. In the late 1960s company and state strategies worked in parallel. By 1967 Ford felt strong enough to attempt a major overhaul of labour relations, just as Wilson and Castle were drawing up plans to confront unofficial strikers.

In late 1967 the NJNC accepted a fivefold job evaluation exercise for all jobs. Previously jobs were grouped as 'skilled', 'semi-skilled', 'unskilled' or 'women'. Each was to be evaluated in accordance with 28 job characteristics organized around five new grades labelled from A to E. The negotiations lasted a year with tens of thousands of working hours lost and scores of disputes jamming the grievance procedures.

One such grievance concerned the Category B regrading of the Dagenham women machinists, instead of the

Category C they requested, and the 15 per cent less they were to receive compared to men on the same grade B. Having lodged requests for reassessment, the seamstresses spent months being ignored before finally walking out on 7 June 1968. The Halewood machinists followed, and car production halted.

The women stayed out for a week, famously having tea with Barbara Castle, before voting to return with a deal that immediately increased pay to 8 per cent below that of men, rising to the full B rate the following year. Category C status only came after a further six-week strike in 1984.

It is difficult to separate the seamstresses' battle from the wider Dagenham industrial politics of the time. Between February and March 1969 Dagenham workers, including the machinists, played their part in the first national stoppage across the whole Ford UK estate – unfinished business in earlier regrading battles which helped sink Harold Wilson's reform of labour relations.

1969

The 1969 strike signalled a move away from the shorter, sporadic local actions characteristic of the 1960s towards the more protracted industrial battles of the 1970s. Under the new leadership of Hugh Scanlon and Jack Jones in the Amalgamated Union of Engineering Workers (AUEW) and the Transport and General Workers' Union (TGWU), greater emphasis was placed on internal democracy and shop steward power. The strike exposed the changing Wilson government approach towards labour regulation as the dispute headed to the industrial courts and Labour towards defeat at the polls. The industrial battles between Ford and Scanlon and Jones played out as the same union leaders struggled with Castle and Wilson over *In Place of Strife* – published literally weeks before the action started.

The origins of the dispute lay in the 1967 regrading fights, with stoppages and overtime bans continuing through 1968, building pressure on the NJNC. A 'working party' came up with a pay deal with productivity strings and penalty clauses modelled around those contained in *In Place of Strife*. The White Paper proposed new government powers to settle unofficial disputes and enforce penalties for non-compliance. Days later, Ford proposed an Income Security Plan but with a six-month disqualification rider for any 'unconstitutional' activity or strike action. This move to buy out unofficial union activity and re-establish management control of production echoed government plans revealed in the White Paper for the rest of industry.

The Dagenham convenors were the first to hear the contents of the package. Despite AUEW opposition and TGWU abstention, it was accepted by the other NJNC unions on 11 February. The move was celebrated by press and politicians as a sign of growing industrial maturity which, alongside Castle's legislation, would resolve unofficial disruption for good. In Ford it became an issue of shop floor power against that of the company, NJNC and government.

Within a week unofficial action closed Halewood. Almost immediately it was officially sanctioned by the new leadership of the AUEW and TGWU, but not the majority of NJNC unions. Then Dagenham walked out.

The company vowed to keep the plants open and took the two unions to court to bind them to the agreement, just as Castle sought to bind the labour movement to new constitutional arrangements to regulate unofficial action. The court granted Ford an injunction, although the strike was called off when the company weakened the penalty clauses and agreed a reconstituted NJNC, including greater AUEW, TGWU and plant representation.

The government climbdown took a few months longer. In early 1969 Castle pressed ahead with an Industrial Relations Bill but, under lay pressure, the TUC remained unprepared to discuss unofficial action. Within a few months it became apparent Castle and Wilson did not have Cabinet support. On 19 June Scanlon and Jones offered the government a ladder to descend; a 'binding and solemn' agreement that the TUC would attempt to resolve unofficial disputes. Later, in April 1970, a tepid Bill was unveiled, but the government was defeated before it even received a Commons second reading.

The 1969 strike helped defeat *In Place of Strife* and set the stage for the battles of the 1970s. A ten-week parity strike by 50,000 Ford workers in 1971 was only resolved when Jones and Scanlon called a halt with a two-year pay deal. Heath's 1971 Industrial Relations Act, which included new laws covering unfair industrial practices and legally binding agreements overseen by a specialist Industrial Relations Court, pushed similar reforms to Castle and met with similar results. Political reaction to the Act together with the miners' strike and three-day week culminated in a 'who governs Britain?' election and Labour's return to office.[15]

The Labour government of 1974–9 walked away from *In Place of Strife*. It re-embraced the voluntarist tradition and sought to enact the Donovan programme through five basic statutes: the Trade Union and Labour Relations Act (TULRA) 1974 and its 1976 amendment, together with the 1975 Employment Protection Act and Sex Discrimination Act, followed a year later with the Race Relations Act. This substantial wide-ranging programme inherited from Donovan offered employment protection against unfair dismissal and against discrimination on the basis of sex, race, marital status and pregnancy; a union recognition procedure; and a series of other collective rights, such as time off for union representatives, and created new tripartite machinery, including ACAS.

Yet corporatism failed to deliver the industrial peace the Oxford School had hoped for. Yet again it was the Dagenham Ford workers leading the pay round who successfully took on both the company and government's 5 per cent pay norm in 1978. This gruelling two-month struggle broke the government pay policy and set up the public sector strikes and winter of discontent which culminated in another Labour election defeat.

Through the late 1970s elements of the political right broke ranks with post-war corporatism. Such opposition had existed before Thatcher – *A Giant's Strength* in 1958 had attacked the perceived privileged position of unions since 1906. Yet by 1979 the corporatist state was now being systematically undermined with the wide-ranging intellectual challenge we now describe as 'Thatcherism' in reaction to widespread industrial militancy, the breakdown of pay policy and recurring stagflation. Thatcher's embrace of economic liberalism signalled a reorientation away from the concerns of post-war bipartisan corporatism. Pluralist recognition of a discernible 'labour interest' was replaced with the active atomized consumer inherited from Neo-Classical Economics and deployed with a new language of popular capitalism – the origins of what is now described as 'neo-liberalism'.

3

Miracle Cures

Stepping Stones

On 14 November 1977, from his home in Great Waldingfield, near Sudbury in Suffolk, John Hoskyns, later Head of Policy in Downing Street,[1] circulated a landmark political report entitled *Stepping Stones*.[2] Written in collaboration with Unilever's Norman S. Strauss, the document sought to reorder domestic politics through a reassessment of labour regulation drawn straight from textbook neo-classical economic theory. The paper, including introduction, summary, six sections, handwritten diagrams and appendix, came to just 69 pages – the boiled-down conclusion of months of strategic discussion at the heart of an emerging, new radical right.

The scale of ambition was clear from the first few lines: 'national recovery will be of a different order from that facing any other post-war government. Recovery requires a sea-change in Britain's political economy'. The goal was not election victory but a transformed nation; success defined not by the usual calculus of electoral politics, nor even a landslide, but 'something morally and economically better'. National decline was the fault of the trade union movement, the organized industrial working class. Their overriding objective was to identify in the minds of the people union responsibility for the 'sick society'. Their task was to ensure the 'electorate is offered conflict about the status quo' to overhaul 'the union movements' political and economic role'.

The texture of the document is raw, confident and ideological, of a type rarely seen in politics, a point it drily concedes: 'today's pressures are often themselves caused by lack of strategy'.

Moral and economic transformation had several 'sub-objectives': ending inflation, correcting inflationary expectations, cutting back the state's tax take, overhauling pay bargaining structures, restoring investment: but they were all second-order concerns when compared to confronting union power. Evolution – 'satisfactory' progress – was insufficient; revolutionary zeal was required. Accommodation with organized labour, conservative collusion with post-war corporatism, was now considered a sell-out and recipe for managed decline. The task was to instil 'a sense of shame and disgust with the corrupting effects of socialism and union power – class war, dishonesty, tax fiddling, intimidation, shoddy work – the "sick society"'. It will require 'systematic and painstaking effort' to confront a malign union movement, years later famously framed as the 'enemy within'.

The objective was radical disruption – 'discontinuity' – with 'leadership at a premium'. Trade union power, where 'Jim's Britain is a sick Britain', threatens 'the family, individual freedom and the social market economy'. Modern conservatism must 'govern through discontinuity'.

The appendices explained the task: to shift from 'fear' of unions to 'hatred' to build 'hope' and 'courage'. The authors alight on a phrase Thatcher used months earlier in an interview with Brian Walden[3] – 'let the people speak' – to confront mob rule. They sought to 'institutionalize legitimate means for breaking rules'. Rereading the document today, descendants of Thatcher appear to have inserted 'European Union' for 'trade union' to define the modern villain or 'other'; the inhibitor of national freedom and prosperity. Today the chaos of Brexit will supposedly upend managed decline and offer a new Britain endorsed with reference to the 'will of the people' in a parallel of the disruption envisaged in 1977.

Stepping Stones is reminiscent of an earlier document; a companion piece that helped to frame British neo-liberalism. Two months after Thatcher became leader of the Conservative Party, in April 1975, Keith Joseph presented *Notes toward the Definition of Policy* to Thatcher's Shadow Cabinet.[4] In the first few pages, Joseph outlines the politics of what became known as Thatcherism, through an initial self-critical assessment of Conservative involvement in post-war corporatism, a tradition he believed lacked leadership and became a slave to consensus: 'we competed with the socialists in offering to perform what is in fact beyond the power of government'. Morally, 'by ignoring history, instincts, human nature and common sense, we have intensified the very evils which we believed, with the best of intentions, that we could wipe out'. It is time to turn the page: 'now is our opportunity, perhaps our last, to make a new start . . . if we are willing to turn away from our mistakes'.

The document lacks the tight focus of *Stepping Stones*; the unions figure but do not occupy the definitive role of the later document. This reveals the political evolution of the project, one expressed with growing clarity around labour regulation. This focus on labour was to become the historic gateway to embed Neo-Classical Economics within an entire liberal political philosophy and programme of government.[5]

Neo-Classical Theory

The academic economic community didn't foresee the 2008 crash, although few have acknowledged any guilt.

They missed it because economics has become a remote, calculating 'science' cut off from society. Referring to this isolation the great American economist J.K. Galbraith once remarked that 'specialization is a scientific convenience and not a scientific virtue' and a 'core source of error'.[6] How do we make sense of this division between economy and society, where the 'dismal' science has been removed – abstracted – from the realities of how people live and work? Why is this hardly ever discussed, when it imperils people caught on the wrong side of these economic busts?

Since the later stages of the nineteenth century, mainstream economics has contracted into a rigorous model of price allocation within a pure exchange system, in reaction to the profound industrial and social upheavals of the time. Since the 1870s modern Neo-Classical Economics has built a model of exchange that initially isolates then aggregates market transactions determined by crude assumptions regarding human nature, our desires, preferences and ways we act in the pursuit of utility.

The 'marginalist' economic revolution contained several fundamental breaks with CPE. Social relations between people are reduced to technical ones between isolated calculating economic agents. The currency of economics, the value of things, was reset away from people building things and into the realms of individual subjective preferences. It produced a theory of value based on utility under the guise of 'science'. Study of the economy became separated from the life, times and experience of people. Historically specific forms of social and economic organization are considered natural and beyond political contest. Yet this new 'science' was a deeply political reorientation.

This reformation was a conscious attempt to define the limits of state intervention and resist escalating pressures for social and economic reform with the industrial and political mobilization of the working class. In such a demanding environment strict laissez-faire political economy offered diminishing returns. Economics successfully changed the conversation by retreating from attempts to reconcile classes in search of a new individualized science of society expressed as a strict determination of market prices.

This reset begins with individual economic agents entering the marketplace equipped with their own fully informed preferences in terms of what they wish to consume and how they wish to allocate time, for example between work and leisure. These preferences are exogenous, they stand outside of the explanatory power of the framework, and in the eyes of the committed remain immune to criticism.[7] It is then assumed that these economic agents – people – act rationally in the context of scarcity, irrespective of whether they produce or consume things. Prices are set by aggregating numerous acts of rational exchange: on the demand side by the marginal utility derived from the consumption of a unit of goods, and on the supply side by the relative scarcity of the good in question.

How does this approach understand work? The production of things, arranged within the firm, is a consequence of these basic assumptions. The theory of rational exchange is extended into a theory of production, a technical relationship between what goes into the firm and what comes out. Work becomes the bridge between these factors of production and outputs. Labour is considered one of these predetermined fixed factors – a trade-off between our preferences for work and leisure.

The production function is the academic device that identifies and calculates the contribution of various factors of production in the final output. It is again a margin call. An array of factor prices translates into efficient outcomes determined by their relative productivity at the margin. Human labour is a fixed input into production; technology is seen as another exogenous constant and beyond the formal explanatory power of the framework. Given this array of assumptions, the firm is naturally assumed to be technically efficient. Maximum output is produced from any likely combination of inputs.

The neo-classical framework, the model that shapes our

lives, tends not to consider the organization of work as significant given the technical symmetry between inputs – factors of production – and outputs. This symmetry is dependent on certain assumptions regarding rational economic activity and the human condition. Marginalism holds an internal coherence in the way it regards the numerous individual actions which collectively form the economy. It remains abstract, asocial and institution-free: a pure theory of exchange relations.

People are hired dependent on their marginal productivity – if their predetermined productivity exceeds the wage. The labour market is characterized by voluntary participation and mutual benefit. Theoretically the worker is hiring the employer just as much as the employer is hiring the worker!

Is the work we perform predetermined – a fixed factor of production – or does it have to be organized, directed and controlled? Can our work be reduced to the status of all other non-human inputs into the production function? Is the labour market characterized by a seamless series of rational transactions? Is participation a purely voluntary activity, an individual trade-off between wages and the disutility of work?

Earlier we described the model as ahistorical, noting it cannot consider the time dimensions by which people form economic relations. Nor does the model deal with most contemporary institutional features of the capitalist economy, other than through reference to 'imperfections'. Yet it contains implicit assumptions about technological and, therefore, historical change. It assumes the factory system and the capitalist division of labour are the natural, most efficient way to coordinate acts of market exchange given the technical requirements of available factors of production. The model of perfect competition falls prey to technological determinism in its denial of the need for power and control as motivating forces in the creation of the factory.[8]

So basically, this revolution assumes everyone to be a

price taker and technological change occurs at an exogenous rate. Initial endowments are taken as given and everyone acts rationally in the context of full and perfect information. We are consequently left with technical relations between things upon which we derive quantitative solutions to outputs, inputs and prices – all of which have equal status. The functional interdependence of the model leaves very little to explain.

Earlier economists assumed class reconciliation through the expansion of production and the distribution of the proceeds of growth; for later economists these tensions emanating within the organization of work are assumed away. The firm – and the organization of work – became a 'black box' – beyond understanding or explanation. Compared to CPE, value was removed from the organization of work and into the domain of personal preference. The scope of economic enquiry dramatically truncates, from one anchored around social and class relations within the division of labour to a technical relationship between inputs and outputs and questions of economic exchange. These shifts marked a watershed in social and economic theory and offered a robust justification for capitalist society. The focus of economic study – for political economy the question of growth through distribution – is replaced by the question of economic allocation through the process of exchange.

Late nineteenth-century instability created a crisis in political economy and transformed the notion of value from one grounded in human labour and the production of things into the domain of metaphysical individual assumption and desire. Economics could become what Karl Korsch once described as a 'disinterested scientism'.[9] It explains why mainstream economics and politics are so uninterested in the organization of work and human labour. It is not oversight; they are placed beyond theoretical range and decoupled from politics. In so doing they attract a different type of economic and political attention.

Subjective preferences determine patterns of ownership

and the distribution of resources. Wealth and poverty func-
tionally reflect the rational pursuit of one's innate desires
and tastes. From now on there is no Trinity Formula, only
the link between rationally acting individuals; the principles
that determine whether an individual is a worker, a capitalist or landlord are the same. The model is not repudiated
if capitalism fails to fully correspond to abstract theory;
it instead suggests capitalism has yet to perfect its own
institutions. The role of politics is to remove impediments
and shape society around this abstract theory of individual
exchange, including the operation of the labour market,
expressed so clearly in the pages of *Stepping Stones*.

Shock Doctrine

Over a period of 18 years successive Conservative
governments sought to confront organized labour and
dismantle labour market regulation and employment
rights equipped with a language of freedom, liberty and
justice in pursuit of an abstract economic ideal. The institutional architecture of post-war corporatism – including
the NEB, MSC and NEDC – was dismantled or significantly curtailed. A supply-side revolution geared up as
the Fair Wages Resolution was abolished and the young
removed from wage council coverage, but the real target
was the unions.

The 'Prior Act' – the 1980 Employment Act – extended
the tortious liability of the unions over industrial action.
The voluntarist principle that had shaped the history of
British labour law was under attack. The 1982 'Tebbitt
Act' further restricted the definition of legitimate industrial
action and union protections. They were to be 'wholly or
mainly' linked to – rather than 'in contemplation or fur-
therance of' – a trade dispute. It also enabled the selective
dismissal of strikers and restricted the closed shop.

The voluntarist gateway – the unique British system of
negative immunities rather than individual and collective

legal rights, secured early in the century with the Trades
Disputes Act – was stripped back to allow the sequestration
of union funds. Acceptable strike action was narrowed by
excluding secondary and overtly political strikes. Pickets
were limited, union disciplinary action in support of strikes
banned alongside official union support for illegal strikes.
All strike action had to follow a tightly regulated balloting
procedure adding to both cost and complexity. Unions
were banned at GCHQ. The legacy of 1972 and the mass
picketing of Saltley Gate, closing a Birmingham fuel storage depot and securing victory for the National Union of
Mineworkers, was avenged after a 51-week miners' strike
throughout 1984 and 1985. All this as 20 per cent of manufacturing output and 2 million jobs were lost between
1979 and 1981. Unemployment peaked at 3.3 million in
September 1985.

The proportion of employees in unions crashed from
56 to 31 per cent. In the private sector, workplaces with

Union membership over the last century mirrors the income share of the top 1 per cent
Union membership (1,000s) and share of income going to the top 1 per cent (%), 1918–2014

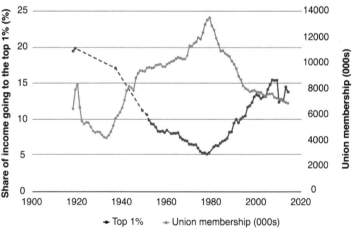

Figure 1. Union membership 1990–2014

Source: IPPR, 'Power to the People: How Stronger Unions Can Deliver
Economic Justice', 10 June 2018.

recognized unions and twenty-five or more employees halved from 50 to 24 per cent and the proportion of employees protected by collective agreements collapsed from around 55 to 25 per cent.

Britain became more unequal. Post-war trends that had seen income inequalities incrementally fall were suddenly reversed. In the battle between capital and labour, labour lost. Graphically it can be expressed in an inverse relationship between the wealth of the top 1 per cent and levels of union membership (see figure 1). Union decline kicked in as incomes shifted to the top 1 per cent with extraordinary speed. Management prerogative was restored through neo-classical concerns to individualize the employment relationship, aided and abetted by a new labour relations language – we were now all in it together.

Unity

Unitary models have developed to operationalize the abstract neo-classical model of the harmonious employment relationship. These reject the inevitability of workplace conflict and believe employment relations remain inherently cooperative. Conflict is irrational given the overriding mutual benefits inherent in the labour market transaction. Conflict can arise but is considered the result of inefficient information exchange, with the onus placed on management to reorganize and resolve the causes of any discontent.[10] Alternative sources of authority and power at the workplace, for instance through independent trade unions, undermine the unity of the organization and need to be challenged and eliminated. Such assumptions operate behind the backs of many forms of political and organizational theory.

The classical scientific management techniques pioneered in the car plants by F.W. Taylor, 'Taylorism', sought to secure rigid control through task fragmentation. The belief was that ruthless organizational efficiency established through mechanization and rigid hierarchical discipline was to the benefit of all who work in the enterprise. The 1980s saw the development of more sophisticated management practices to secure the same unity of purpose and secure neo-classical outcomes. Human resource management provided subtler methods to cultivate the cooperative work environment. Emphasis is placed on nurturing the collaborative organizational culture, often with the aid of interventions such as appraisal and personal development techniques, individual contracts and performance-related rewards. The human relations school is another unitarist variant with its emphasis on methods to provide for human self-fulfilment at work and enhanced mutual satisfaction between employee and employer against the backdrop of harmonious employment relations, for example in the work of organizational theorist John Child.[11] Here the emphasis is on fostering techniques that involve employees themselves in the organization and regulation of the workplace. The 1980s saw a neo-classical onslaught backed up with growing unitarist sophistication defeating post-war pluralism and its identification of the labour problem.

Unity in Dagenham

The Dagenham militancy regularly on show throughout the post-war period dramatically receded as the Thatcher reforms kicked in. The company learnt from past mistakes and gradually reasserted management prerogative of the labour process. More and more Ford cars were either assembled abroad or built with foreign components. The company developed the 'world car' – made up of a compact, low-weight, simplified body shell. Plants increasingly resembled one another, allowing production to be shipped easily between plants. Consequently, the company was in a strong negotiating position to play off individual countries against each other in bidding wars for new investment.

When Ford announced the Bridgend Engine Plant in late

1977, hundreds of millions of pounds in grant was supplied by the government and Welsh Development Agency following tough company demands. TGWU national officer and lead union negotiator at Ford Ron Todd was to complain that they didn't want any of the Dagenham labour practices brought into the plant.[12]

Union power was in steep decline as employment in the sector dramatically contracted. Between 1971 and 1981, employment in the main car producers had fallen from 304,000 to 196,000. A 1980 TUC study noted that the sector accounted for 23.4 per cent of all redundancies between October 1980 and February 1981.

In terms of plant labour relations, the company demonstrated it had learnt from decades of disputes and sought to involve and consolidate the unions in the management process, very much in the manner Donovan had proposed years earlier, but in the 1980s aided by subtle unitarist HR techniques. Following changes in the aftermath of the 1969 strike, the NJNC was gradually expanded to include all the plant convenors. The company offered support for union officers and facilities in the plants. More computer control and automation were introduced, further wresting control of the labour process from the workers. In the early 1980s Ford experimented with newly fashionable forms of 'worker involvement' throughout the estate, including production 'quality circles' first showcased in the successful Japanese plants alongside more direct individual communications with the workforce. Company personnel management strategy had successfully progressed beyond the simple principles of 'Taylorism'. Tens of thousands of jobs were lost across East London as management regained control of the labour process.

Miracle Cure?

From the mid to late 1980s, it was commonplace to hear vainglorious talk on the right of an economic transformation as evidenced by manufacturing productivity data, the 'judge and jury' of Thatcherism.[13] Economic commentary suggested a productivity breakthrough, even a 'miracle'.[14] On one level the figures were impressive (see table 1).

Table 1. Key labour market indicators: 1979–1989

Year	Output per person	Manufact- uring output per person- hour	Average weekly earnings	Retail price index	Real earnings
1979	89.5	79.3	53.9	60.0	89.8
1980	87.6	78.1	65.0	70.6	92.1
1981	89.2	82.2	73.3	79.1	92.7
1982	92.6	86.6	80.2	85.8	93.5
1983	96.7	93.3	87.0	89.7	97.0
1984	97.6	97.7	92.2	94.3	97.8
1985	100.0	100.0	100.0	100.0	100.0
1986	103.0	103.3	107.9	103.4	104.3
1987	106.0	109.8	116.3	107.7	108.0
1988	107.6	115.8	126.4	113.0	111.9
1989	107.2	120.0	137.9	121.8	113.3

Index numbers, 1985 = 100
Source: National Institute Economic Review

The data suggest substantial productivity rises, especially in a steeply shrinking manufacturing sector, alongside rises in earnings and inflation, the latter constraining movements in real wages. Yet talk of any 'miracle' was overblown. Despite relatively low labour costs, British labour productivity was so poor that our comparative productivity position in terms of value added per person remained very weak. Measured in terms of total factor productivity, the 1980s re-established the trend in UK post-war performance – a comparatively weak trend. Given the significant output loss between 1982 and 1989 and the shedding of 2 million manufacturing jobs, the recovery in output with a significantly reduced workforce suggested work intensification through the supply-side reforms of the Thatcher era rather than more profound technological restructuring.

Those that follow the neo-classical faith would agree that we can refer with precision to an efficiency gain if output increases with the same levels of input. They should also agree that the issue is more complicated if additional output is secured through increasing the consumption of inputs. If, as suggested above, the supply-side reforms may have raised levels of output as a result of more input expenditure (through labour intensification) rather than productive or technological innovation, then the verdict on economic efficiency is by no means clear.

Even ignoring these points, productivity levels weakened following the 1988 budget deflation and the recession of the early 1990s put paid to talk of any 'miracle'. Rhetorically, the neo-classical revolutionaries saw off the classical concern with the labour problem, and unitarism might have slain pluralism, but this dramatic lane change hardly cured our long-term productive weaknesses. Enter New Labour.

4

New Labour

Neo-Classical Labour?

New Labour is not easy to pin down. From the left a general criticism suggests it simply built on a neo-liberal inheritance – by extending the market into public services, rejecting redistribution as an essential target of public policy in deference to corporate power, with multiple privatizations and much more. Pushing on with Tory reforms exposed a liberal economic worldview. This line of attack is all a bit too easy. First and foremost, neo-liberal political economy asserts the state inhibits efficient market transactions whereas New Labour retained a benign belief in state intervention.

In its approach to the labour market, New Labour is again regularly described as neo-liberal in the sense that it retained the political representation of labour established with the New Right. This suggests Blair and Brown bought into a neo-classical supply-side agenda, and accepted wholesale Conservative reforms. Again, this popular riff remains one-dimensional in addressing labour regulation after 1997 – although Blair didn't help. In appeasing the powerful, he regularly appeared ready to embrace such an inheritance.

Prior to taking office, Blair implied he would retain the Tory reforms. Famously, during the 1997 campaign he announced in the pages of *The Sun* that with him in power the UK labour market would remain the least regulated in Europe. Critics often tend to use this campaign statement as a literal assessment of the Blair period – even before he began his term as prime minister!

Without doubt the new government lacked the clarity and intellectual coherence of earlier Conservative and Labour approaches to labour regulation, and internal tensions persisted because of this. Some argued for robust employment interventions and a revival of Donovan-era pluralism. Others, who in the past might have been their allies, instead ruled this out given the changed context of globalization. Instead, they sought to maximize the welfare of the working class through tax reform rather than the extension of collective bargaining. A different group embraced a European route to legislative reform that challenged traditional voluntarism. Then there was Blair himself, latterly driven more by electoral calculus than policy and yet, as we shall see, committed to an approach to knowledge work that dramatically reset the whole debate around Labour, class and work regulation in ways that were subsequently passported onto the Corbynite left. Therefore, whilst Thatcher cast a long shadow after 1997, we require a more nuanced approach to interpret labour regulations under New Labour. It is necessary to unpack the enduring influence of the politics of Donovan, prevailing Treasury thinking, the gravitational pull of European labour regulations and the particular stamp of Blair himself. These, I will argue, were all elements that inform today's 'labour problem' and political stasis.

Donovan's Early Influence

With rear-view vision, many remember New Labour as an uncomplicated continuance of what went before. However, there were notable interventions influenced by traditional pluralist concerns to regulate labour and some successes should be noted. There were early attempts to build a new 'industrial relations settlement' through new bilateral CBI and TUC dialogues. These helped shape the government's 'Fairness at Work' agenda and subsequent White Paper which set the terms of the 1999 Employment Relations Act.

The independent Low Pay Commission was a clear tripartite expression of industrial pluralism, established on a non-statutory basis in July 1997 and consolidated into legislation through the National Minimum Wage Act 1998. The Commission's board reflected the model of social partnership that inspired it – made up of three employer representatives, three representing workers and three 'winger' experts.

Some saw in these early moves the suggestion of a more enduring model of corporatist 'social partnership'. A few years earlier, then Shadow Chancellor John Smith had privately advocated a tripartite National Economic Assessment within Labour's Economic Policy Sub-Committee, although seen off at the time by so-called Shadow Cabinet 'modernizers'. In government Ian McCartney's job description changed from Minister of Employment to Minister of Social Partnership, yet he attracted little support and with the departure of TUC leader John Monks to the European Trade Union Confederation (ETUC) in 2003, the shutters came down on any remaining possibilities for the development of a more formal tripartite economic dialogue.

In terms of labour law, early whistle-blower protections and a reduction of the unfair dismissal qualifying period to a year signalled a Donovan-era inheritance. So too did the 1999 statutory union recognition laws, rights to be accompanied in disciplinary and grievance procedures and the introduction of the Union Modernisation Fund. All sought to facilitate collective bargaining and effective dispute resolution. New protections in lawful industrial action against dismissal and discrimination on grounds of union membership, non-membership or activity followed, as did blacklisting and strike ballot reforms and enhanced rights to workplace training.

Whilst the pluralist tradition helped shape policy in Labour's first term, any real influence disappeared after 2001. A review of union recognition procedures was promised but little came of it. In 2004 some minor technical alterations to prevent 'union busting', protect strikers, adapt the right to be accompanied, amend balloting procedures and halt far right entryism were introduced. Yet after the first term nothing helped to spread collective bargaining coverage or union density. The reason was that advocates of industrial pluralism couldn't rely on the support of the traditional utilitarian right wing within the party whose leadership, now occupying 11 Downing Street, had switched tactics in order to maximize working-class welfare – an under-reported switch with epic repercussions for British class relations, social and European stability and politics across both the British left and right.

Treasury Utility

Within the Treasury, and anticipated by Bill Clinton's New Democratic policies, there was a working assumption that declining real wages across the West would be one of the immediate effects of globalization and heightened international competition. As such this necessitated a policy response that would question Labour's traditional approach to labour market interventions. Modern economic realities meant traditional labour market regulation could price people out of work and inhibit domestic growth.

Whilst the traditional Labour right wing within the government sought to bolster working-class disposable incomes, the means to achieve this diverged dramatically from post-war approaches to labour regulation. No longer was this to be pursued by extending collective bargaining and voluntarist tripartite remedies, but through new tax credits funded by a growth engineered through an alliance with finance capital. Policy focus was consciously directed away from traditional party concerns with strengthening a 'labour interest' and more with remedial cash transfers to alleviate the declining living standards of the working class, especially its young families and older pensioners. This redistribution worked in tandem with a refinancing of public service safety nets, achieved through asserting an 'end to boom and bust' and henceforth sharing the proceeds of growth secured by a lightly regulated compact with the city. It translated into an internal hostility to anything beyond limited labour market intervention. The many advocates of this approach argue that it helped secure sixty quarters of economic growth and three massive majorities in 1997, 2001 and 2005.

Rights, Equality and Europe

Traditional pluralism was in retreat not just due to a lack of Treasury support but because of the effects of European integration. Since Jacques Delors visited the TUC Congress in 1988 at the high point of Thatcherism, a gradual reorientation had been underway as the labour movement rushed to embrace the European 'social model' and interventions that rested uneasily with the history of voluntarism and British labour law. An imported tradition sought to regularize employment standards through recourse to individual and collective rights rather than immunities, including the 1998 and 2007 implementation of the Working Time Directive and rights to information and consultation. Consequently, labour reform was gradually subsumed within a wider European regulation of labour.

Recent Brexit debates have revealed the long-term effect of this subtle historic reorientation on the left, subcontracting domestic political contest over labour issues to transnational judicial oversight. Over recent years many 'remainers' have argued that the European courts and a vaguely defined Continental social model account for the hard-won rights of British workers imperilled with Brexit. In Labour today the defence of employment rights is seen as a compelling reason to remain in the EU. Yet the reality is more complex. Over many years the European Court of Justice[1] has appeared intent on dismantling the type of social model embraced by the British labour movement in a period of 1980s powerlessness. Meanwhile, the way European legislation has been introduced in law has been shaped by domestic politics to either go beyond the European proposals or limit their application, such as over the regulation of working time or codetermination. It was never a simple story of enacting European law into domestic legislation or accepting the decisions of the European courts. However, the emerging role of international labour rights challenged the unique traditions of domestic labour regulation.

Labour's 'family-friendly' or 'work–life' balance initiatives are a case in point. Rights to flexible working for parents, guardians of young or disabled children, those with caring responsibilities and adoptive parents, together with rights to paid and unpaid maternity leave and paid statutory paternity leave, can all be situated within progressive equalities thinking inherited from the Donovan era. Yet they can also be seen to reflect the failure of voluntarism and autonomous collective bargaining to deliver genuine equality and help account for a gradual embrace of more legalistic and international approaches to justice across the left.[2]

Blair

Then there was the Blair effect. Once he became prime minister, polling dominated policy. Ideas became the raw material to achieve political position and engineer the retention of power. Such a strategy brought to life Schumpeter's famous dictum that the core of democracy lies in the 'competitive struggle for the people's vote' in a similar form that the capitalist seeks to exchange commodities in the marketplace.[3] Votes are the form of exchange, policies the commodities and elected office the derived profit. This is a more effective way to inspect the neo-liberal underpinnings of the Blair administration than actual policy: in the market for votes rather than ideas and what Blair meant when he frequently talked about 'what works'.

There was no a priori hostility to the state, rather its use tended to be calibrated for the purpose of winning the votes of those that mattered – swing voters in swing seats – to reproduce Middle England political domination, Blair's marketplace. New Labour's originality lay in the method by which policy was constructed by focus group participants in order to render intelligible such a political strategy.

Labour regulation helped define Labour after 1997, but in opposite ways to the industrial pluralism of post-war Labour Britain. Blair's 'Young Country' could no longer countenance such old-fashioned approaches to regulation. Throughout the dark troubled decades of opposition, Labour was associated with failed periods of economic intervention, tax-and-spend welfarism and union militancy. The defeat of 1992 pushed policy towards a 'supply-side socialism' to remedy polling negatives. This trend rapidly intensified with Blair's ascendance to the leadership in 1994. A few ideologists stepped up and sought to reinterpret a radical political repositioning with reference to a revolution in economic relations, which was luckily occurring just as Blair became leader, freeing him from the imperatives of both labour regulation and party history.

Knowledge Work

For many around Tony Blair the growth in *knowledge work* meant an end to the 'old' economy, 'old' labour and the case for regulation. Beginning in 1994, ideologues within New Labour developed a narrative predicting fundamental changes in patterns of work and foresaw a coming revolution in economic relations. Just like today, they cited technology as a driver of change in work and employment; a new *knowledge-based economy*, a vision of what working life in the twentieth century could be.

Such an analysis of globalization and technological change might have offered a haunting spectre of disappearing employment opportunities in the traditional sectors of the economy, and pointed to growing insecurities, widening social divisions and under-employment in communities like Dagenham, which any Labour government would be duty-bound to correct. Blair rejected this analysis whilst remaining optimistic about the prospects for working life in the twenty-first century.

Charles Leadbeater, an adviser to Tony Blair, argued that 'smart' technologies and globalization were driving the emergence of a new economy, centred not on heavy industry and the production line, but on the exploitation of so-called 'intangible assets'. 'The real wealth-creating economy is de-materialising,' he wrote. 'The private and public sectors are increasingly using the same sorts of intangible assets – people, knowledge, ideas, information – to generate intangible outputs, services and know-how.'[4]

The old structures and labour markets associated with large public and private sector organizations were allegedly being replaced by networks of independent, small-scale companies. Old hierarchies and the conflicts between worker and boss were to become a distant memory. Future economic prosperity was to be driven by the production of knowledge and these 'intangible' assets, whilst traditional manufacturing and heavy industry declined. In short, the distinction between worker and employer was withering away, an interesting echo of the basic neo-classical theory of the employment relationship, but not an embattled Thatcherite one.

Leadbeater's highly influential analysis echoed earlier concerns of US industrial sociologists such as Michael Piore and Chuck Sable, who pioneered the 1980s 'flexible specialization' diagnosis of the emerging crisis in Fordism. This literature sought to account for the crisis through changing patterns of consumption and argued that future successful firms – and countries – would be those that reacted to this crisis through the introduction of what became known as 'flexible specialization' in production – the efficient use of all-purpose microelectronic production technologies. Small firms rather than large conglomerates would be the new market leaders of the future as new technologies made small batch production cheaper. Small firms that were less bureaucratic, more agile and more responsive to changes in market conditions would prosper, partly through new flexible methods of design and inventory control, but also the close personal relations existing within the modern firm.[5]

The idea of new 'knowledge work' ended the case for regulation. Dehumanized physical toil was becoming technologically obsolete. The slogan 'education, education, education' captured a new tech-savvy, meritocratic rethink that focused on investment in human capital to ensure people were equipped for the technological complexities of this new economic world, best reflected in the 1998 'Knowledge-Based Economy' White Paper.

Closing-Down Sale – Everything Must Go

British car plants didn't fit into this shiny vision of 'new knowledge' work. They belonged to the 'old' economy and held painful memories of 'old' Labour's failed past interventions – a world of 'Red Robbo' and Dagenham militancy that had dragged down successive post-war Labour governments. When, during the early years of New Labour, the same factories – in Longbridge and East London – faced closure, Blair sought to manage the transition to his envisioned sunny new economic uplands through training and financial support, rather than saving jobs and the plants.

In May 2000, following months of speculation, the closure of Dagenham car production was finally announced. It meant that after 69 years, no Ford cars would be built in the UK, despite annual sales approaching 450,000 and a 20 per cent market share. The new Fiesta once promised for Dagenham was instead to be built in Germany, where the company had just 6 per cent of sales.

The unions were adamant Dagenham was targeted because of the comparative ease with which British workers could be made redundant. Union leaders claimed Dagenham was a more efficient plant than Cologne, averaging 24.4 hours to build a car compared to 25.3 hours in Germany. Weak British labour laws tipped the balance against Dagenham and British workers.

The announcement followed months of secret talks, including meetings between Tony Blair and Jack Nasser, head of Ford global operations, at Downing Street, and frequent phone calls between Blair and Nick Scheele, the chairman of Ford Europe. Downing Street officials had met car union leaders separately to discuss the proposed closures.[6]

Tony Blair said the government would help those put out of work. 'We will be there to help with money, investment and advice for anyone who does lose their job', he said. The number of redundancies at Dagenham was scaled down from 3,000 to 2,000 to defuse anger. Payoffs of up to £55,000 were offered to assembly workers to encourage them to go quietly. Notices pinned on walls of the Dagenham plant by workers read: 'Closing-down sale – everything must go.' Strike ballots were sent out in October, but the threats came to nothing because so much government and company money was thrown at the problem.

The government feared ending car assembly would provoke a wave of strikes leading to further cuts in Ford operations throughout Britain. Blair was desperate to avoid a repeat of the political fallout from BMW's earlier decision to pull out of the Rover plant at Longbridge, threatening some 20,000 jobs in the West Midlands, which had blindsided his new government. This time closure announcements had to be managed properly and the community softened up with months of press speculation.

Ford sugared the pill by also announcing heavy investment in engine production at the plant and extensive reskilling plans funded by the Department of Trade and Industry (DTI) and London Development Agency. Three and a half years later Blair was in Dagenham to open the new Centre for Engineering and Manufacturing Excellence, which his government had part-financed, and the new Dagenham Diesel Centre. Car assembly had ended, closure had been managed and new training and welfare opportunities were made available.

Blair and Brown United

Overall the Treasury and Downing Street – with support from the DTI – tactically aligned to resist attempts to contest the character of work performed at the point of production and redirect attention onto supply-side reform and aggregate market outcomes. Throughout, the government appeared to prosper. Growth was assumed to be locked in, driving welfare transfers to the poor and refinancing public services. On the surface the strategy was a success. Brown and Blair jointly managed a period of sustained growth between 1997 and 2008. In 1999 the system of tax credits was introduced which, by the time Labour left office, accounted for 1.9 per cent of GDP. Under Labour, spending on public services increased by an average 4.4 per cent a year in real terms compared to a 0.7 per cent average between 1979 and 1997. Yet work and labour remained decoupled from politics within both party and government, upending the priorities of labour history. At the time these were considered positive outcomes – no return to 'boom and bust' and no return to the industrial tensions that bedevilled Labour throughout history. What was there not to like?

Yet whilst initiatives to regulate and dignify labour were consistently resisted or diluted, tax credits allowed employers to free ride and wages flatlined, which, paradoxically – just like in the Thatcher era – arguably served to intensify work at the expense of technological innovation and the development of 'good work'. These issues festered and, after a financial collapse, became cruelly exposed in shifting patterns of working-class political affiliation reflected in four Tory victories – despite a decade of austerity – and in Brexit.

Ignored Not Wiped Out

Yet even at the time, hiding in plain sight, labour market statistics revealed a story at odds with the Blair narrative of dematerializing labour and unencumbered portfolio working. By the end of Labour's first term the trends were clear. Successive Labour Force Surveys pointed to only a slight rise in those jobs considered white-collar and above – up from some 35 per cent to 37 per cent of the total stock of directly employed and self-employed occupations – in the UK labour market in the decade after 1992. On the same statistical series, manual workers still accounted for a relatively stable 10.5 million workers – approaching 40 per cent of total employment. If you were to add in clerical and secretarial work, then the traditional labour force stood at some 15 million – approaching two in three jobs.

By 2001 the growth areas in the economy included a slight rise in computer managers, software engineers and programmers. Yet the real growth had been in the long-established services of sales assistants, data input clerks, storekeepers, receptionists, security guards and the like. Alongside this, there was a massive expansion in cleaning and support workers in the health and education services and beyond, and increased work among the caring occupations – such as care assistants, welfare and community workers and nursery nurses. There was no revolution in the demand for labour – the key growth areas were in traditional, often low-paid jobs, many of which were carried out by women.

In contrast to the language of Labour's knowledge revolution, analysts started to note the emergence of an 'hour glass' economy in the UK.[7] On the top half of the hour glass there had been an increase in high-paid jobs, performed by those with significant discretion over their hours and patterns of work – these might be described as knowledge workers. However, of more empirical significance was the growing trend of low-paid, routine and much unskilled work in occupations pre-eminent 50 years before. Labour just did not want to acknowledge what appeared in clear sight.

Policy persisted to be framed by assumptions of a certain technological destiny, not just questions of labour law and regulation but also concerning the demand for graduates and for funding higher education. A belief in future knowledge work informed the radical New Labour objective of securing 50 per cent school leaver participation in higher education. In the battles over top-up fees in the second term, Education Secretary Charles Clarke stated: 'Demand for graduates is very strong, and research shows that 80% of the 1.7 million new jobs which are expected to be created by the end of the decade will be in occupations which normally recruit those with higher education qualifications.' Yet such assumptions ignored that a high proportion of this related to NVQ Level 3 and not higher education qualifications. Once this extra growth was taken out, then the figure for new jobs by 2010 requiring a degree shrunk to 55 per cent. This did not include demand for so-called replacement jobs – which stood at five times as high as for new jobs.[8]

In 2001 when the government's own statistics were broken down, they revealed that by 2010 the figure for those in employment required to be first degree graduates or postgraduates would be 22.1 per cent. In other words, 77.9 per cent of jobs would not require a degree. Even at the high point of New Labour we were witnessing an ever-clearer polarization within the labour market. On the one hand, a primary labour market – or the knowledge-based economy – covered about 21 per cent of jobs. On the other, there was an expanding secondary labour market where the largest growth was occurring in service-related elementary occupations, administrative and clerical occupations, sales occupations, caring personal service occupations and the like. The political strategy of New Labour was focused on the top end of this hourglass – and a neglect of the vocations and labour market realities underneath – with disastrous political consequences for the left over the following two decades as the working class deserted the party.

The 'Labour Problem'

Under New Labour, trade union density continued to decline from 31 per cent of all employees in 1997 to 27 per cent in 2009, and in the private sector from 20 per cent to 15 per cent. The proportion of employees who had a purely non-union channel to management rose from 41 per cent to 46 per cent between 1998 and 2004 (having been 16 per cent in 1984). The proportion with a purely union channel (24 per cent in 1984) fell from 9 per cent to 5 per cent in 2004. The expression of worker discontent had been largely individualized. In short, New Labour – and the last vestiges of the Donovan tradition – failed to halt union decline and correct the long-term shift in the balance of economic forces between capital and labour.

So, overall, labour market thinking under New Labour was a complex story. The party of organized labour didn't simply succumb to the power of capital and economic liberalism, although Treasury hubris before the crash of 2008 suggests otherwise. The government was preoccupied with overall labour market statistics rather than the character of the work performed, driven by Treasury welfarism and Downing Street determinism. Some twenty years on we can see the consequences of such neglect in studies such as James Bloodworth's *Hired*, in work that reveals the social and psychological consequences of the degradation of work. Tory legal restraints on strikes, over balloting, picketing and secondary action were maintained for similar reasons, plus the presentational optics. All of which drove a belated political reckoning within the party and informed Corbyn's accession to the leadership. Yet the popular political backfill that New Labour was simply neo-liberal is far from the full story.

In New Labour's first term we saw pluralist attempts to regulate labour. Any influence quickly declined, however, to be replaced by a gradual reorientation towards more legalistic and procedural routes to remedy labour market inequalities, at the expense of political traditions historically suspicious of both the courts and individual rights. This is part of a wider social democratic reorientation towards legal intervention and judicial interpretation, a more robust embrace of rights-based models of justice. This will redirect our attention from the simple economic regulation of labour towards competing theories of justice, which dominates the second half of the book.

Some have argued that New Labour's policies contributed to an improving productivity performance, through growth of education, support for innovation and tough competition policy.[9] Yet nearly a decade after New Labour was ejected from office, productivity is once again back on the agenda. Since 2008 there has been an unprecedented fall in UK productivity. This, when considered alongside poor wage growth and price rises, has produced a profound deterioration in living standards. Consequently, household income growth has been worse than during the early 1990s recession following the UK crashing out of the Exchange Rate Mechanism (ERM) in September 1992. Despite a variety of post-war attempts to overcome our comparative weaknesses, informed by various approaches to the regulation of labour, today talk is of a productivity 'puzzle' rather than 'disease' or 'miracle'.

Against a material backdrop of ten years of virtually zero productivity gains, households appear to have boosted incomes by working more hours in more jobs and with more intensity. Immediately before the virus derailed the economy, employment was three percentage points higher than in 2007, while the average working week was unchanged at 32 hours, having fallen by an average hour every four years over the past century. It appears that working with an increasing amount of effort whilst experiencing heightened insecurity is a modern reality for a significant, growing part of the labour force and remains a key part of an enduring labour market puzzle.

The most recent evidence from the Skills and Employment Survey 2017 identifies several productivity drivers. These cover employee autonomy, influence and discretion over their labour, voice at work, responsive management, the prevalence of initiative taking, innovation, high-impact suggestion making and high-productivity-enhancing jobs. Since 2006 these productivity drivers have all become less prevalent, precisely at a time when productivity growth has been sluggish. These results remain robust across occupation, education and industry. British workers are working harder, faster and to tighter deadlines than they did in the past. If effort were all that mattered, we would expect productivity to be booming, not stagnating.[10]

All of this before the full shakedown from a global pandemic. We appear in desperate need of a new approach

to managing the labour market. On the left we were sup-
posed to have been offered one with Corbyn, one more in
keeping with Labour history. In reality, as we shall now
discover, what was really on show was more of the same
rather than the promised break from New Labour.

5

A Return to Marx

The decade-long 'puzzle' of stagnating productivity, alongside concern for flatlining wages, modern work quality and enduring austerity, has seen a rejection of traditional postwar approaches to labour regulation. In place of industrial pluralism or the concerns of both the New Right and New Labour, in recent years radical new approaches to automation and postcapitalism have emerged that claim a Marxist inheritance rather than one from CPE or the neo-classicists. Yet the true significance of this renewed interest in Marx, and how it has influenced modern debates on the future of work and the wider renewal of the left, can only be genuinely understood by locating this new literature within the history of Marxist thought and precise, highly questionable, theoretical assumptions it makes regarding the nature of capitalism. This will gradually become clearer but requires an understanding of key concepts in Marx's own work and, since his death, their subsequent usage within Marxism, and how they link to our earlier discussion of Ricardo and the practical political effect of certain assumptions relating to value and labour. Such an approach uncovers serious difficulties for significant sections of the modern left.

Modern Utopia

Chronocentrism is a term first coined by Jib Fowles to describe 'the belief that one's own times are paramount and that others pale in comparison'.[1] It can imply a certain chronological snobbery; that a specific period of time – usually the present – holds greater significance than others. It can present as a form of generational egotism in overvaluing the significance of one's own age cohort and their contribution to history. Politics attracts the evangelizing, optimistic chronocentric, confident in their ability to navigate the future, powered by determinism. We detected this in the knowledge work assertions of New Labour. Historically the condition affected Marxism with its understanding of how technology shaped history and assertions of revolutionary immanence within capitalism. Yet Marxism is once again on the move. Since the global economic shakedown, it offers a hip antidote to the sell-outs supplied by technocratic social democracy and the brutality of neo-liberalism.

Today, a major intellectual renewal is underway on the left.[2] It is young, energetic and tech-savvy. It maintains a rich, radical intellectual heritage within the European left, embraces bold new ideas, and is well organized and networked. It is fast becoming a new political movement best captured in influential articles and books discussing 'accelerationism', 'postcapitalism' and even 'fully automated luxury communism'.[3] It is a literature that within a short space of time mainlined into left thinking, especially in debates about UBI, given the lifestyle potential offered by epochal technological change.

The origins of much of this new thinking lie in the radical politics of fifty years ago. Post-workerism or *postoperaismo* emerged out of the 1960s Italian workerist movement – *operaismo* – powered by a critique of the centralized, orthodox Italian left. The latter sought to build a politics autonomous from traditional forms of representative democracy. The emphasis was on direct, subversive action at the workplace. By the early 1970s, workerism had evolved into post-workerism, incorporating a wider conception of anti-capitalist struggle beyond the immediate form of capitalist exploitation at work, as a response to the automation of the Turin car plants. It also contained a corresponding redefinition of the working class, triggered by technical change towards one of the 'socialized worker' – all those contributing to the reproduction of capitalist labour power, for example students, housewives, etc.

The 'post-workerist' reorientation on the radical left was popularized by Michael Hardt and Antonio Negri in *Empire*, a work highly influential among those inspired by the anti-globalization movements, and later the post-2008 crash Occupy protests and militant campus agitators of the last decade.[4] This theoretical inheritance was present amongst the younger democratic elements within the Momentum organization and parts of what was the Corbyn leadership team. The hallmark of this loose grouping is their utopian, optimistic reading of the potentialities of a 'post-work', 'postcapitalist' future. This new thinking imports into the radical left a very specific, optimistic reading of technological change and its opportunities. It asserts an imminent transition to a vaguely defined era beyond capitalism. The era of postcapitalism beckons as the capitalist relations of production cannot manage the epochal shifts in the forces of production that we are currently experiencing. Once again work and labour are 'dematerializing'. For a growing movement that claims allegiance to 'Marxism', it is worth dusting down what this means.

Value Theory

Marxist economics is regularly packaged within the tradition of CPE. Both contain theories of value based on human labour and both are concerned with class dynamics within

society. Yet bundling up Marxism within CPE misreads
Marx's approach to work and labour. This mistake, as we
shall see, has significant political implications which have
distorted the history of the left and continue to reappear
today. It is a misunderstanding that fails to recognize the
fundamental differences between Marx's Labour Theory
of Value (LTV) and the embodied labour times approach
of Smith and Ricardo we discussed in chapter 2.[5]

The LTV dominates Marx's writings, yet his account of
the exploitation of labour under capitalism and transformations within the system is a source of such confusion
that it can upend his understanding of history and technological change. This is not simply an abstract academic
misrepresentation. Disguised within certain technical economic categories are fundamental political questions that
span the last 150 years, and which re-emerge even today to
disfigure the left. These political tensions and controversies
reside within the LTV and require a certain appreciation of
Marx's method.

Marxist economics begins by separating the use-value
of a commodity from its exchange value, and the unique
properties of human labour. Marx identified four elements
to labour – private, social, concrete and abstract – which
pertain to all forms of society and anchor his diagnosis of
capitalist exploitation.

Under all types of society, production occurs to create
use-values, things that give satisfaction to their users.
Under capitalism, goods are produced primarily as bearers
of abstract labour and are represented as exchange values
in the market. The common property of commodities is
that they are the products of human labour.

Marx distinguishes between the concrete and abstract
labour within a commodity and the private and social
dimensions of this labour. Concrete labour refers to the
precise types of labour that create use-values; independent
production without social mediation. Abstract labour is
homogeneous labour in a collective general sense. Social
labour relates to the objective social form taken by labour

in any society. Under capitalism, concrete labour is 'privatized' and the social aspect is 'abstracted'.[6] Under any form of social organization social labour dominates private labour. Under capitalism the distinction between social and abstract labour is wiped out, with abstract labour giving social labour the dimension of quantity.

This understanding of labour separates Marx's economic method from other traditions. Power relations, conflict and control at work are neither ignored nor institutionally resolved through growth. They remain central concerns because of the unique characteristics of labour. Human labour is best understood not as a predetermined thing but as an indeterminate, transhistorical capacity which takes different forms under different forms of production. Marx diagnosed how under capitalism this potential itself becomes a commodity – the commodity *labour power*. Within the capitalist labour process human labour power can create value for the owner of this potential over and above the wage it was sold for before being set to work.

For Marx, capitalism cannot be understood without an appreciation of how the labourer sells his or her capacity to work and is rewarded with a wage to help reproduce this potential. The capitalist purchases this capacity alongside other commodities which are worked on within production to create other commodities. Capital is made up of means of production, constant capital, which transfers its value in production, and labour power, variable capital, which creates more value within production. Surplus value is the difference between the value of labour produced by the worker and the value of their own labour power. Exploitation is the product of a social process by which labour power, once commodified, is set to work under a historically determined authority relationship which may be more or less precisely specified. Marx's analysis of the capitalist labour process therefore echoes his approach to the commodity.[7] On the one hand, it produces use-values; on the other, it creates value over and above the value of labour power. Abstract labour is the sole source of value.

Important implications flow from this approach. Under capitalism, social relations dominate material production and reflect the dominance of value – objectified abstract labour – over use-value – concrete, private labour – captured in Marx's exposition of the commodity. Exchange value is the form of representation of materialized abstract labour, objectified in the marketplace when products become commensurable as commodities. Exchange is not simply a technical thing – *it expresses the social organization of labour in production*. The measure of value is the measurement of abstract labour – average units of labour socially necessary to produce the commodity.

In contrast to CPE, the LTV is not a theory of price formation, as the exchange value is the 'form of appearance' of the indeterminate labour potential having been set to work; it is a method of understanding and not an empirical calculation. Ricardo's theory falls apart when price and value diverge, whereas Marx distinguishes between value and exchange value or price.

This specific theoretical turning point has shaped politics on the left for 150 years. Distinct highly contested readings of value within Marx's work have informed alternative approaches to technological change and the nature of capitalism. Fundamental schisms within the history of the left flow directly from what appears as a rather technical approach to human labour and once again reappear today as Marx has been rediscovered since the financial crash, especially in debates around the future of work.

To briefly sum up and reinforce the point, Marxism considers capitalist production as the unity of material production, the labour process, and the production of certain social relations, where labour power is consumed in the creation of value. Under capitalism, it is the latter process, of value creation, which is dominant.

Critically, when Marx considers production relations, *he is not* considering material production as such – private labour in the production of use-values – but rather the social relations within which production takes place.

Famously he stated in the preface to *A Contribution to Political Economy*:

> in the social production of their life, men [*sic*] enter into definite relations that are indispensable and independent of their will, relations of production ... The sum total of these relations of production constitutes the economic structure of society.[8]

The volumes of *Capital* essentially develop this basic method to understand capitalism as a socio-historic representation of this dominance which he elaborates through two sets of couplets: the formal and real subsumption of labour and relative and absolute surplus value through their effects on the organization of production.

But here is the odd thing – and why we needed to plough through this. Despite the significance of these concepts in Marx's own work, after his death they met with very little attention within Marxist scholarship itself! This was partly a product of political defeat in the West,[9] in particular the defeats of the proletarian insurgency in central Europe in 1918–22 and of the late 1930s Popular Fronts, and subsequent failure to convert the resistance movements into durable left political projects after the Second World War. Two other factors account for this intellectual retreat: the systematic Stalinization of Russian society, and the post-war economic buoyancy of Western market economies. Consequently, in the West, Marxist analysis shifted into abstract discussion within university philosophy departments and between 'structuralist' and 'humanist' traditions, discussed in part II, at the expense of either the LTV or practical consideration of workplace affairs and the realities of capitalist exploitation.

Consequently 'economistic' positions came to dominate Marxism. Historical materialism became a technological conception of history, especially within the politics of the Second International and in the work of key theorists such as Karl Kautsky and Georgi Plekhanov. The political imperative was to attempt to establish the objective, scientific status of the theory and the inevitability of success.

Orthodoxy therefore asserted that the historical progress of the material productive forces conditioned the actual social relations of production, *and not the other way around*. This inversion of Marx's actual method borrowed from the Marxism of Engels and philosophical assumptions of dialectical materialism, with an emphasis on a 'dialectics of nature' and the laws that govern the natural sciences. Technology is seen as the motor of history; it shapes production. The forces of production – technological change – develop exogenously and overturn Marx's own emphasis on the social basis of class struggle.[10]

The consequences of this economistic reading of the LTV now come into focus. First is a tendency to consider history in a linear fashion, as the relentless development of productive capacity and the neglect of actual political struggle and agency. History unfolds. This is the hallmark of a dominant, scientific technological determinism within the history of Marxism and the authoritarian character of much of the left. This reappears today within a left technological utopianism. Second, it tends to neglect the study of work within the history of Marxism – where exploitation and class struggle originate. Marxism became an economic science, but one that actually neglected economics in favour of philosophy, bent through deterministic readings of Marx; one that also neglected the workplace, an extraordinary about-turn given that Marx's method hinged on the labour process as the site where value was created!

Other popular criticisms of Marxism are best understood through this lens. In general, the LTV has been criticized from two standpoints, external and internal. External criticism tends to point to its illogical foundations when compared to the benefits of later neo-classical thinking.[11] The basic attack often centres on seeing labour as the sole source of value given that other common properties to commodities exist which can impart value, such as scarcity. Of course, if value is seen as aggregated embodied labour times, collapsing the difference between abstract and concrete labour, then this is indeed a valid criticism.

In contrast, internal critics have sought to strengthen the overall Marxist approach by asserting that abstract labour is average labour in terms of skill and intensity, as embodied labour within a commodity, rather than abstract labour where social labour takes the form of an abstraction or alienation from its concrete aspects within production.[12] In this defence of Marx, the concepts of value and surplus value become redundant; analysis shifts from consideration of surplus, concrete, labour and class struggle to distributional struggles over this surplus. This is the form of Marxism we have described as 'Ricardian' given that it suggests an embodied labour time approach to value similar to the one discussed in chapter 2 as advocated by David Ricardo. The consequence of this politically is an emphasis on distributional struggles across society rather than one embedded in the character of employment. Once again from within the Marxist tradition the tendency is to neglect workplace issues. Consequently, the regulation of work, including the forms taken by labour power, the organization and control of the labour process, and the politics of technology were all neglected within Marxism.

Work and Marxism

Marxist analysis draws on a diagnosis of unresolved class conflict originating in the nature of the employment contract and patterns of ownership in capitalist societies. The commodification of the human labour potential – labour power – lies at the root of this conflict and the gearing of the system to create surplus value through the exploitation of the wage labourer.

It is therefore extraordinary that so little work within the Marxist tradition focused on the actual dynamics of the employment relationship under capitalism. For a while that changed following the publication of Harry Braverman's epic *Labour and Monopoly Capitalism* (LMC) in 1974 and the development of what has come to be known as 'labour process theory' within industrial sociology and industrial relations analysis.[13] The Ford Motor Company is once again centre stage.

For Braverman, scientific management, or 'Taylorism', represented the clearest practical articulation of the coercive imperatives of accumulation to undermine the dignity of human labour – 'nothing less than the explicit verbalization of the capitalist mode of production'.[14] The labour process was being deskilled through technological change, the fragmentation of tasks and the erosion of craft traditions, thereby removing personal discretion from the hands of the worker. Work in the twentieth century was being relentlessly degraded by the way 'Fordist' technologies ensured systematic, centralized control over production. Braverman rationalized Taylorism: 'Its role was to render conscious and systematic, the formerly unconscious tendency of capitalist production. It was to ensure that as craft declined, the worker would sink to the level of general and undifferentiated labour power, adaptable to a large range of simple tasks, whilst as science grew, it would be concentrated in the hands of management.'

Criticism of Braverman's work regularly led with charges of technological determinism. By interpreting his deskilling thesis as an empirical study of work degradation rather than a long-neglected creative application of the LTV, this form of criticism misreads the true significance of his book. Braverman succeeded in reorienting Marxist analysis away from the dominant deterministic readings of how the forces of production condition social relations at work. He specifically stated, 'technology, instead of simply "producing" social relations, is produced by social relations represented by capital'[15] and rejected determinism: 'How is the labor process transformed by the scientific and technical revolution? – no such unitary answer may be given.'[16] For Braverman, social relations in production determine the forces of production and not the other way around, due to the indeterminate nature of human labour.

Braverman's work inspired a belated reorientation on the left to correct a long-standing neglect of work and employment relations. A 'labour process' literature was born providing an alternative to orthodox approaches to work organization. The indeterminate labour potential replaced the predetermined productivity assumed by orthodox economists. Beginning in the late 1970s, inspired writers such as Michael Burawoy, Andrew L. Friedman and Richard Edwards created a rich literature on the radical left analysing the historical development of the capitalist economy through the study of workplace relations and methods to control the production process.[17] Yet gradually over time this literature lost its radical edge and any remaining links with the LTV. 'Labour process' debates shrank, tending towards more empirical study of job design and technical questions of human resource management.

For a short period, Harry Braverman reset Marxist analysis of work in line with Marx's own method. It did not last. One area where the radical methodology did remain was in consideration of gender division, labour market segmentation and work organization. Here radical and socialist feminist analysis of patriarchy contributed a literature on gender and employment beyond affirmative action and equal opportunities, discussing the wider gender relations that reproduce labour power, the role of housework, and the definition of work itself. Yet it wasn't until the financial crisis of the late 2000s that Marxist interest in work futures was to substantially re-emerge and with it the baggage of earlier 'Marxisms' obsessed with technology and not politics derived from a highly precise reading of Marx and his understanding of human labour.

Reading Marx

Technological determinism within scientific Marxism arose from an inversion of Marx's own method, thereby prioritizing the forces over the relations of production. This involved an embodied labour time theory of value which we labelled Ricardian in its approach to Marx; one which tends to promote linear interpretations of history. Such orthodox Marxism has now reappeared within fashionable parts of the tech utopian left, through the appropriation of Marx's *Fragment on Machines* – quite literally a couple of pages pulled from his *Grundrisse* notebook that predated the volumes of his masterwork *Capital*.[18] The *Fragment* is a key text because it is the route by which the value theory of Marx has been reconsidered through a Ricardian lens at the expense of his later completed work. In so doing it has built an overconfident diagnosis both of the state of modern capitalism and of the future strategy for the left.

The *Fragment* foresees a future where the direct labour input within capitalist production declines through the development of the forces of production and automation. This allows modern commentators to connect their approach to value theory based on the amount of concrete labour invested in commodities with the overall trajectory of capitalism. Their approach to value informs a theory of history determined by embodied labour times.[19] This literature assumes that, for Marx, what gives a commodity value is the amount of labour directly embodied in the creation of the commodity. Technological change ensures that this direct labour is in decline; it is being dematerialized. This theoretical backdrop then allows them to assert the creation of modern wealth independent of labour and consequently suggest a 'knowledge-driven route out of capitalism'.[20]

Many key points made by Mason in his important book *PostCapitalism* carry traces of the Italian left that sought to make sense of the late 1960s automation in Turin car factories with reference to embodied labour expended within production, and the implications of this for class composition inside and outside the plant. Later, under Negri's intellectual leadership, the *Fragment* attained its full significance in the way it suggested Marx foresaw technological change displacing labour – and literally capitalism – due to a specific approach to removing concrete labour within the production of commodities. In a *Guardian* piece, Mason wrote: 'There is, on the left, an implicit understanding of political philosopher Toni Negri's claim: that the "factory" is now the whole of society and the subject of change is everybody – especially the networked youth'.[21]

This whole political reorientation owes more to Ricardo than to Marx. Mason makes this clear in the pages of *PostCapitalism* when he writes that 'a commodity's value is determined by the average amount of labour hours needed to produce it . . . We can express it in money'.[22] Here, just like for Ricardo, the LTV is considered a theory of price. In the next paragraph he explains that: 'Two things contribute to the value of a commodity: (a) the work done in the production process (which includes marketing, research, design, etc.) and (b) everything else (machinery, plant, raw materials, etc.). Both can be measured in terms of the amount of labour time they contain'. Consistently Mason consciously or otherwise defines himself firmly within the embodied labour time tradition. This then shapes his whole approach to technological change and the transition to an era of postcapitalism.

Mason's thesis of epic change – and prognosis of future strategy for the left – hinges on his use of the *Fragment*. Over eight pages he sets up both his presentation of his core *PostCapitalism* thesis as well as a specific reading of the LTV in his sixth chapter.[23] He concedes that the *Fragment* challenges every other reading of Marx, basically leading to the creation of capitalist wealth independent of the labour expended. This theoretical trigger point allows Mason to then suggest the 'networked youth' are destroying capitalism as the information economy is not compatible with the market economy. At a stroke, the 'holy trinity' of Classical Political Economy in the creation of value – of land, labour and capital – is replaced by people, ideas and things. Capitalism is thereby dramatically dissolved as the labour process disappears.

To recap. If value is seen as aggregated labour times, then the qualitative difference between abstract and concrete labour under capitalist social relations is lost. Value is simply seen as the aggregation of those use-value-producing dimensions of human labour, calculated prior to the specifically capitalist processes where labour is rendered social. Here the concepts of value and surplus value become redundant – analysis shifts to questions of concrete labour – and political struggles become distributional struggles. What were initially technical debates within value theory have today come to define the character of the modern left – with disastrous consequences.

This approach provides the postcapitalist radicals with the theoretical foundation for resetting the base of the left away from any discernible 'labour interest' or working class, through a method endowed with an anti-humanist technological determinism. This approach to labour and value builds a seductive belief in imminent revolutionary change and in a new political cosmos built around a networked youth. We see erected a comfortable worldview predicting immediate transition to a vague postcapitalist nirvana through the liberating highway of automation. For these modern Marxists the site of political struggle is removed from the workplace into wider society as the wage–labour relationship offers diminishing returns as we hurtle toward a 'fully automated luxury communism' of the present. What flows from such an audacious rethink? The desire for Universal Basic Income becomes self-evident; such a policy can even help speed up the process by which labour can 'dematerialize'. Why campaign to defend work which is inevitably disappearing or even fight factory closures? Why resist the employment consequences of a global pandemic which might accelerate moves to an automated future? Why ally with a trade union movement that seeks to defend what you desire to overturn? Profound consequences follow from rejecting a 'labour interest', henceforth considered at best political nostalgia, at worst reactionary.

The reverberations that follow this textual reading of Marx and a consequent desire to accelerate the substitution of human labour – the working class – with technology en route to 'communism' are immense. Henceforth, the base of the left becomes a new urban, networked educated youth, instead of the historic class base of left politics.

Traditionally, the left's 'base' was the working class. Various pluralist and socialist traditions all accepted the centrality of the capitalist wage–labour relationship in diagnosing political struggle. This operated as a shared reference point across the left; a political docking station for assorted left traditions based on a shared understanding of such a discernible labour interest. This collective base camp is now threatened as fashionable left theorists have taken it upon themselves to rewrite the entire purpose of left politics.

For example, Paul Mason is clear when he suggests that 'a new strategy must be based on the realization that Labour's heartland is now in the big cities, among the salariat and among the globally orientated, educated part of the workforce'.[24] He explicitly identifies this as the 'new core of the Labour project'. The new base, according to Mason, is formed of 'networked individuals' – echoing the left-wing sociologist Manuel Castells and his understanding of 'radical, horizontal social movements'. This suggests to Mason links with 'small, often socially-conscious, entrepreneurs and large numbers of people who work in a globalized corporate environment' – arguments reminiscent of the likes of Leadbeater, Piore and Sable – and Blair – just a few years earlier.

In a more recent *New Statesman* piece on the left after Brexit, Mason is upfront when he argues that 'the old relationship between the urban salariat and the ex-industrial working class *has inverted* . . . Labour is the de facto party of the urban salariat. Its heartland is Remainia'; a structural shift which offers a much-vaunted 'new politics'.

This is a big deal. A basic misreading of Marx is used as the basis to redraw the character of left politics. Marx's

Fragment bolsters a crude determinism which, like most orthodox Marxism, translates into a cold utilitarianism where human beings are considered little more than carriers of the economic forces driving history; agency and politics evaporates.[25] Overly optimistic prognoses laud the possibility of substantial change within the context of a crisis-ridden capitalism. But the fashionable salience of the slender few pages of a text as slight as the *Fragment* rests on an old-fashioned understanding of concrete labour as the direct source of value that Marx refuted in subsequent pages of *Capital*. The implication remains that we must adapt our politics to match the march of the machines, rather than vice versa.

This ignores – at a huge cost – what machinery means for workers engaged in production in capitalist societies where our human creative essence is subordinated to other ends. Politically, orienting a programme for the left around errant theoretical derivations from disputed fragments of Marx's work and empirical speculations of a future that may or may not come to pass is unwise and potentially dangerous.

Assertions regarding dramatic technological transition rest uncomfortably alongside our comparative economic weakness and the presence of a modern productivity 'puzzle' – and the necessity of rebuilding work following a pandemic – which should all direct attention towards real problems and issues in the modern organization of production. Ironically enough, many of today's radical left appear the natural descendants of the 'Third Way' to which the wider project of Corbynism was posed as the alternative, both modern movements being driven by highly specific readings of technological developments within modern capitalism.

Part II: The Ethics of Labour

In part I, we looked at how various economic theories of labour helped shape post-war British political history and compete today to interpret the future; a journey from a 'disease' to a 'puzzle' by way of a 'miracle'. Before the pandemic struck, we had reached a point of stasis with a political class bewildered at enduring productivity short-falls and incapable of rethinking the politics of work. Both the social democratic and radical left had subscribed to forms of technological determinism[1] and post-war plural-ism had been eclipsed. On the right the supply-side reforms of the Thatcher era failed to deliver any enduring uplift. Post-Brexit, the new Conservative Party leadership were searching for a 'blue-collar' reset before the virus struck, whilst much of the party remains beholden to liberal eco-nomic purity. Meanwhile informed commentary appears obsessed with epic rupture through imminent automation despite record employment levels, albeit much of it precar-ious. Even before the pandemic there was a growing need for something different.

External shocks create political possibilities. The finan-cial crash of 2008 could have triggered a reckoning with globalization but instead led to years of Tory ascendency and a decade of austerity. The Brexit interregnum was resolved decisively by the Conservatives with the left again failing to show up. In the aftermath of pandemic, people desire a different truth, one preoccupied less with the cost of living and more attuned to a different type of living.

Rebuilding our society and economy will require a different form of moral and political leadership. In the second part of the book we readdress the labour question in a different way, from the perspective of ethics and justice.

Across both left and right, politics tends to offer a vision of human beings as little more than carriers of economic forces that propel history forward. Post-pandemic, these look underwhelming. In this section we replace the three economic approaches to labour discussed in part I with three traditions of justice. These traditions seek to maximize either human welfare, human freedom or human virtue. This alternative approach will allow us to subsequently return to the economics of labour and reassess the contribution of the Oxford School by locating it within a neglected ethical socialist tradition.

Chapter 6 begins with a discussion of the nature of labour and rethinks both the history of Dagenham and the history of work. We then specifically address questions of human dignity and labour and draw on a short Polish film that has showcased these themes. Chapter 7 pauses the argument. Our approach to the dignity of labour might be derailed in two obvious ways: first, if we discover that people don't desire work with intrinsic meaning, if for instance people simply instrumentalize their work; and second, if this interest in work will simply be overtaken by technological events that affirm the end of work. Chapter 7 therefore inspects two literatures: the first, what we know in terms of how we feel about our work; the second, what we know will happen to work in the future. The final chapter offers a wider discussion of justice and the history of socialism, seeking to rehabilitate a neglected socialist humanist history and return to certain themes from part I in our understanding of economics and politics and the ethical concerns of the Oxford School.

6

Dignity

Dagenham Labour

Dagenham is situated 13 miles east of Charing Cross. Historically an ancient agrarian village, later a civil parish in the Essex Becontree Hundreds, it remained undeveloped until 1921, when London County Council began constructing the vast Becontree estate, which saw rapid population growth. It became an urban district in 1926 and a municipal borough in 1938. In 1932 the electrified District Line of the London Underground was extended through the borough with stations opened at Dagenham and Heathway. In 1965 the Municipal Borough of Dagenham was abolished and became part of the London Borough of Barking, renamed Barking and Dagenham in 1980.

In 1931 the Ford Motor Company relocated from Manchester's Trafford Park to Dagenham, having purchased a vast area of marshland in 1924 for £167,700. The site on the southern estuarial edge of Essex offered deep-water port access allowing for bulk coal and steel shipments on a far larger scale than the barges of the Manchester Ship Canal.

On 17 May 1929, Edsel Ford cut the first marsh turf to mark the start of construction. Work continued for 28 months and required 22,000 concrete piles to be driven through the clay to support a factory with its own steel foundry and coal-fired power station.

The estate comprised the Metal, Stamping and Body plant, the MSB, where the frame of the vehicle was pressed from steel and joined, and the Paint, Trim and Assembly plant, the PTA, where the bodies were transferred, painted and fitted, and engines, wheels and transmission assembled. Three other plants supported these two core features: engines, wheels and trim.

The 475-acre riverside site became Europe's largest car plant with 4 million square feet of floor space. The company acquired its principal UK body supplier, Briggs Motor Bodies, in 1953. A £75 million plant redevelopment completed in 1959 increased floor space by 50 per cent and doubled production capacity. At its peak in 1953, 40,000 workers were on site. In total, some 10,980,368 vehicles have come off the line and over 40,000,000 engines.

Yet by 2000 the only Ford produced at Dagenham was the Fiesta. In that year the company took the decision not to tool the plant for the replacement model due for launch in 2002. Vehicle assembly in East London ceased in 2002, but engine output increased in the new Diesel Centre of Excellence with capacity to assemble 1.4 million units a year, more than half of Ford's worldwide diesel output.

In October 2012 Ford announced the stamping plant and toolroom would close the following summer. In June 2019 the company revealed plans to close the Bridgend engine plant, leaving the Dagenham plant with its 2,000 employees as the only surviving UK diesel engine facility – a technology threatened since the September 2015 Volkswagen emissions scandal.

The Public Philosopher Comes to Town

On Wednesday evening on 1 March 2017 in Sydney Russell School Hall, Dagenham, Michael Sandel facilitated a public dialogue on people's attitudes to work and a future without it, in an event recorded for the BBC *Public Philosopher* series on Radio 4.[2] It contained a wide variety of contributions from, amongst others, car workers, fast-food employees, students and railway workers, as well as people employed in a range of white-collar jobs, and included both union activists and managers. The discussion covered UBI and working hours, the role of job guarantees, individual rights and union recognition. The most powerful insights concerned the moral purpose of work, how it informs our sense of a good life and the role employment performs in both the creation and destruction of community; a story intrinsic to the history of Dagenham.

In contrast to what is often quite a cold, statistical literature on the future of work, Sandel managed to solicit a complex story concerning attitudes to our own labour. The contrast between what people wanted and what they experienced, their hopes and lived reality, was at times painful.

With the aid of the audience, Sandel established an essential reality that much work commentary tends to forget, that people's views are complicated. People value good purposeful creative work as a source of meaning in their lives. It can provide independence and identity, and grant personal esteem and contribute to our capacity to flourish and live the life we wish. Conversely, work can also be personally degrading. It can be a source of stress and undermine individual, family and community wellbeing. We can hope for one thing yet experience something quite different. Despite this reality, much modern literature on employment futures tends to squeeze out complexity in a binary debate that considers work as either inherently good or bad.

This tension that Sandel helped explore is often lost in academic and political debate. Much of the literature either holds that work and having a job are good irrespective of content or emphasizes people's frustrations with precarious, degrading, objectively 'bullshit' jobs.

Work can be a source of both hope and humiliation. Simply picking a side, celebrating either the end of work or the maximum number of jobs irrespective of quality doesn't tell us much. Instead, we might wish to organize a society that seeks to create and reward good work and challenge its degraded form and the alienation that comes from it. It is a political challenge. Good work can help to build a good life, but bad work can damage our health, sense of personal standing and overall wellbeing.[3] People can think more than one thing at a time and they can hope for things to be better when they know they are not. Having a bad job doesn't mean you don't value work. This paradox, an apparent contradiction, is played out both in the history of Dagenham and in the everyday lives of its residents.

This idea of paradox helps us appreciate how people can both instrumentalize work – a source of cash – and yet embrace a work-based collective identity and aspire for more personal creativity and freedom, promotion and advancement. It is not a question of work being inherently good or bad: it is the recognition of complexity.

Sitting in the audience with Sandel that night, the discussion was reminiscent of a landmark work in British sociology, Huw Beynon's *Working for Ford*, first published in 1973. The book is an extended discussion of the paradox of human labour and the political struggle to retain human dignity in the post-war Dagenham and Halewood car plants, played out in struggles to control 'speed-up' of the assembly line. For the worker, job control enacted by local steward organization offered greater discretion and autonomy from the supervisor and management. It amounted to organized resistance to the degradation intrinsic to Ford's production technologies. The fight over the organization of production could literally be a matter of life and death.[4]

The assembly line produced feelings of instrumental detachment – the workers felt 'no moral involvement with the firm or any identification with the job', yet such feelings could also shape individual and collective identities through this process of resistance. The Ford production line and wider culture was still influenced by the doctrine of 'scientific management' – Taylorism – conceived in the early twentieth century by Frederick 'speedy' Taylor to organize production into the most routine tasks, thereby removing any human discretion or creativity from the worker. Beynon concluded his 1984 second edition by addressing the tension at the heart of his work:

> This paradox – human potential alongside worry, tedium and despair – is the paradox of our time. It is one that we need to urgently resolve for, in the UK at least, time is getting short.[5]

For Beynon the long-term battle at Ford was to resist the human degradation intrinsic to Taylorism and fight for control over the labour process. This offered the prospect of retaining human dignity through freedom from control rather than safeguarding craft through guild regulation. Over 35 years later, it is a good time to return to this paradox. We can start by rethinking the fundamentals of human labour.

What Is Work?

As a noun, work describes activities that involve mental and/or physical effort to achieve a desired result; as a verb it details the activity undertaken. In physics, work is an energy transfer measured in relation to force and displacement, calculated in joules.

It is not an exclusive human activity. Animals perform activities that can be described as work to feed, house and protect themselves. Work in its most simple sense details how animals act upon nature's raw materials to achieve outcomes.

What distinguishes human labour from the rest of nature? It involves a separation between instinctive acts, or the labour performed by animals, from those imaginatively performed by the human; the intelligent act of work. This distinction between instinctive action and conceptual thought in acting upon nature is the unique human dimension to work.

Work predates capitalism and the market; it existed before the Industrial Revolution. Under all forms of social organization humans seek to creatively appropriate the natural environment in order to sustain themselves. Work is the process of altering natural products and materials to achieve certain outcomes.

How we work today would be unrecognizable to our ancestors. In hunting and gathering societies it was about achieving subsistence. It was through the agrarian and Industrial Revolutions that work became an independent thing of its own; through the separation between work and leisure and the creation of jobs to be performed. Humans established what we understand work to be, including the repetitive, physical work which has dominated human life since the agricultural revolution. Our discussion is about dispossession, how certain social relations separate us from our own labour, a process not intrinsic to work and labour itself. Harry Braverman captured this:

> Freed from the rigid paths dictated in animals by instinct, human labor becomes indeterminate, and its various determinate forms henceforth are the products not of biology but of the complex interaction between tools and social relations, technology and society. The subject of our discussion is not labor 'in general' but labor in the forms it takes under capitalist relations of production.[6]

Our labour is shaped by social relations because of its fluid character; despite what many economists assume, it is not predetermined. In different languages and societies and throughout history, politics, philosophy and religion, this is often expressed by contrasting the interesting and creative with the boring and laborious. This suggests a basic distinction between simple physical toil and that which is personally expressive and self-realizing. Yet physical toil can be just as expressive. In his famous poem 'Digging', Seamus Heaney affirms as indivisible the work of his artisan father and grandfather on their land when cutting the bog and that of his poet self; dignified productive vocations acting on nature, capable of personal expression and beauty, famously concluding:

> Between my finger and my thumb
> The squat pen rests.
> I'll dig with it.[7]

Physical labour can be creative and dignified, rewarding socially useful work. It can also take the form of a 'bullshit' job; degraded and meaningless, without social value. Simply counterposing toil and creativity is not good enough.

The idea of paradox suggests the apparently contradictory forms our labour can take and their political character. Work has a contested quality, a capacity to provide intrinsic personal meaning and wider social use but it can also be unfulfilling and exploitative. Braverman's work is a study of the degradation of work throughout the twentieth century, whereby the guild labourer's control over their own labour was systematically removed by Fordist production techniques, which strip away personal creativity and discretion through 'Taylorism'. It is a process where work becomes less personally rewarding and more alienated under advanced capitalism.

These characteristics of human labour help us understand changing patterns of both work and community driven by the changing demand for human labour and its regulation. It is a contest that can pull together

communities, towns and nations yet also degrade and
undermine collective identities, for example the romantic
working-class pride showcased in *Made in Dagenham*,
compared to the workless decay on offer in *Fish Tank*. The
dramatic arc suggests a modern dispossession within capitalism. It is not linear or predetermined. It is a contested
dispossession where people battle to retain personal and
collective dignity. Historically, capitalism can be understood through this lens of dispossession, in the politics
of enclosure, the exploitation of labour and control of
the franchise; a contested dispossession over community,
labour and democracy. We can label that ongoing active
struggle against dispossession socialism. We will explore
in detail later how it is a socialism very different to those
that approach history and capitalism as predetermined by
technology.

In the winter of 1799, Dorothy Wordsworth and her
brother William settled in Dove Cottage in Grasmere. The
Industrial Revolution had entered its most intense period;
a time of profound social upheaval and economic rupture.
She kept a diary to write about nature but captured other
things.[8] She described her encounters with beggars and
asked about their lives. Where had these sick, destitute and
uprooted people come from? What was the meaning of
the Industrial Revolution?

The causes of pauperism and the general history of the
English working class since Wordsworth can be understood by the way they were shaped by three essential acts
of human dispossession. First in the dispossession of the
people from their land and general basis of subsistence
through the enclosures, standardized in the 1801 General
Enclosure Act, expressed for instance in the poem 'The
Mores' by John Clare:

Unbounded freedom ruled the wandering scene;
No fence of ownership crept in between

Until:

> Enclosure came, and trampled on the grave
> Of labour's rights, and left the poor a slave[9]

Second, in the dispossession of the people from their own labour. The 1834 Poor Law Reform Act established the basic commodity form of the human capacity to work. Paupers remained confined to the workhouse whilst free labourers earned their subsistence by selling their own capacity to labour or face starvation. Third, in the dispossession of the landless from the franchise with the 1832 Parliamentary Reform Act. So began what Karl Polanyi described as the 'double movement' of capitalism.[10] On the one hand, the market destroys old social networks and reduces all human relations to commercial ones. On the other, is the counter-tendency to defend human values and human dignity; the search for community and security. Considered in this way the regulation of labour under capitalism is a contest over the dignity of human labour because of the paradoxical character of our labour; a source of creativity and status yet capable of being reduced to degraded toil. It is a political contest to retain an essential humanity.

Early capitalism was ferocious and dehumanizing; it can be so today. It was a struggle to create the free market in labour and land through enclosure of the common lands which brutalized the peasantry. Resistance was the security found when people joined together and fought for the retrieval of dignity, control and status. Dignity in death itself became a political hallmark of this fight against dispossession and the ways capitalism fell below certain moral standards.

Take the case of the Paupers Grave, one of the most fearful fates of dispossession. Robert Tressell, author of *The Ragged Trousered Philanthropists*, died in Walton in a Paupers Grave, buried with twelve others, and lay undiscovered until 1970. The Paupers Grave was for the destitute;

for those dispossessed. It became a site of profound struggle. It was the Co-operative Society, through the practices of mutuality and reciprocity, that reclaimed the dignity of the person at their death through the socialization – or the sharing – of funeral rights. It is the same today, a contested terrain regarding the dignity of human labour, one intrinsic to the very nature of capitalism. Neither labour, socialism nor history is predetermined.

The history of work is therefore intimately linked to questions of human dignity. Historically the form of forced or coerced labour, such as slavery in Greek and Roman societies, helped fuel colonial successes, yet was systematically challenged on ethical grounds. Work has also been informed by religious concerns regarding purposeful, dignified, indeed spiritual, endeavour, such as the idea of the 'Protestant work ethic'. Both imply an essential humanity bound up with the notion of human labour. Throughout history technological change has been a contest to preserve human dignity as work intensification in the modern factory crowded out human creativity, in effect recreating slavery within an industrial setting given the alternatives of the workhouse or starvation.

The desire to regulate the employment relationship through technological change – over working time, levels of discretion, autonomy, creativity and personal sovereignty over our labour – can therefore be considered as contests over human dignity, identity and community. These are ethical challenges, not just material ones or technical questions of objective economic efficiency. They are not technologically predetermined as much economic literature, across both left and right, assumes. These are political contests in the regulation of labour, the harnessing of technology and the physical architecture of work.[11] What comes into focus is a fundamental division within the left regarding technological change.

As we saw in chapter 5, after Marx's death there was very little analysis of the labour process within Marxism for nearly a century until the publication of Braverman's immense work.

Marxism was seduced by capital's ability to harness science, appropriate nature and stimulate extraordinary productivity gains. This reinforced a misreading of the LTV which considered technology as neutral and interpreted history in linear terms, driven by this independent technological motor. It even led Lenin to embrace the brutal techniques of 'scientific management' pioneered in the Ford plants – as a '"refined brutality" … containing a number of the greatest scientific achievements in the field of analysing mechanical motions during work, the elimination of superfluous and awkward motions, the elaboration of the correct methods of work' in the interests of Soviet progress.[12] Modern techno-utopian Marxism tends to ignore the warnings of Braverman and treads a similar dangerous path. Dagenham's history should instruct us differently.

Early Dagenham Capitalism

The early economic, political and social history of the twentieth century can be understood with reference to emerging mass production and consumption of commodities driven by the technologies pioneered by Henry Ford. In turn, from the 1970s, much academic and political literature has been concerned with diagnosing the transition from the dominant 'Fordist' regime of capitalist accumulation to what is regularly described as 'post-Fordism'.[13] In the Prologue we touched on this in terms of the condition of Dagenham today compared to the dramatic depiction of the 1968 strike.

The story of the Ford Motor Company and the contested regulation of labour within the plants help us understand changes in places like Dagenham or Detroit and provide insight into the purpose of capitalism itself. The history of the Ford Motor Company reveals the antagonistic, brutal character of early twentieth-century industrial capitalism – harsh, dehumanizing work environments regularly referenced in film and literature at the time.

The Ford Motor Company came into being on 18 June 1903. The moving assembly line, and with it the rigid social order we now understand as 'Fordism', was first introduced into their Detroit Highland Park plant a decade later. Further labour rationalization followed the next year with the implementation of the Five Dollar Day.[14] The environment was brutal and authoritarian – discipline was violently enforced by company allies in the police and the city's mob. The company retained its own private police force numbering 3,500 men. In 1931, the same year the first vehicle rolled off the Dagenham line, a Detroit hunger march was ruthlessly repressed with four dead and scores injured.

Just a few years later the 1936 silent comedy classic *Modern Times* written and directed by and starring Charlie Chaplin, showcased how the dignity of the assembly line worker was stripped away through automated 'speed-up', provoking personal breakdown and hospitalization.

Ford also inspired Aldous Huxley's *Brave New World*. Huxley had read Henry's biography *My Life and Work* on a boat to America and portrayed the industrialist as the creator of his imagined dystopia, the 'World State', the product of the social and human re-engineering made possible by his assembly technologies. He imagines a future where the production line extends into automated human reproduction and consequent totalitarianism – characters chant 'Oh my Ford' rather than 'Oh my Lord'. The calendar begins in AD 1908, the year the first Model T rolled off the Detroit line; subsequent years are known as 'Anno Ford'.

Huxley drew on Ford as it emerged as the first genuine multinational company. The writer and philosopher warned against Ford's technological utilitarianism and the scientific threats it posed to both humanity and community, specifically in his hometown, London. The company's so-called '1928 plan' anticipated an operation with three major headquarters – in Michigan, Ontario and England, in Dagenham. The Dagenham plant was formally opened in March 1931, a month before Huxley began to write the book. In it, a future London is depicted as Fordlandia – the 14,000 km² of Brazilian rainforest Henry Ford had acquired in 1928 to supply rubber for his factories and which he imagined would evolve into his utopia in the Amazon.

It was only in 1941, nearly 10 years after *Brave New World* was first published, following years of violent industrial confrontation, that unions were grudgingly conceded at Ford's Michigan headquarters, and only after a 50,000-strong mass refusal to work, with similar numbers voting for recognition shortly after. Even then, before accepting the inevitable, Henry Ford had to be talked down from arming the non-strikers amongst his workforce! Dagenham union recognition was finally accepted three years later and again only after sit-down strikes against the backdrop of the war effort and munitions production. Although firearms were less freely available, management at the Dagenham plant was no less anti-union than at its US parent company. Later still the company recognized shop stewards but only after 11,000 workers went on strike in 1946.

Dignity

We have referred to dignity, but what is it? Can it be defined? Is it useful given that many consider it at best an elusive word? Is it so fuzzy as to be worthless? In a widely read 2003 editorial, 'Dignity is a useless concept', the bioethicist Ruth Macklin suggested her profession reject its use and instead retain the principle of personal autonomy and with it a sense of a shared universal ability to suffer, prosper, reason and choose, such that no human has the right to intrude on the life, body or freedom of another.[15] Yet dignity is a popular word, used regularly by presidents and popes and as an ethical signifier by public and private corporations and charities. President Obama uses the word when advocating global duties in pursuit of international human rights. In 2008, President George W. Bush's Council on Bioethics published a 555-page report entitled *Human Dignity and Bioethics* – although it drew a stinging response from psychologist Steven Pinker, who described dignity as a stupid idea.[16] Pope Francis regularly talks of the irrepressible dignity of every human. The word retains a moral purchase but is highly controversial.

We can identify a version of dignity which originates from Latin notions of worthiness, to describe something concrete achieved in terms of respect and status. Dignity can be taken away with acts of humiliation that affect worth and esteem, both personally and in the eyes of others.

The word also suggests something more abstract and significant, beyond calculation or simple definition, something that we acknowledge when lost; the negation of dignity. This stretches beyond notions of personal and social worthiness and involves a process of dispossession from, or violation of, a deeper essential humanity. It implies a process of reduction, degradation or dehumanization captured both by religious and secular humanist appreciation of some intrinsic human worth and acceptable moral standards. Dignity in this sense has real political significance across both left and right and amongst a variety of spiritual, ethical and human rights traditions.

Human dignity is a central consideration of Christian philosophy. The Catholic catechism insists the 'dignity of the human person is rooted in his or her creation in the image and likeness of God'. In secularized traditions dignity relates to notions of agency and the ability of humans to choose their own actions. This can imply both individual unencumbered liberty and rights, freedoms and a shared state of being that involves obligations in how we live together.[17]

This idea of an essential dignity frames questions of justice – how society should be organized. It implies ethical duties to remedy things or processes that violate dignity – such as genocide, torture, tyranny and exploitation. This in turn suggests that when we recognize and remedy such human – or animal – indignities, we confer a certain dignity on ourselves. An inability to confront such indignities compromises our own sense of dignity – for instance in the acceptability of forms of death, punishment, slavery or abuse. Our dignity is shaped by what we tolerate and what we do not.

This was captured in the aftermath of the inhumanity of genocide and Nazi degradation in Articles 1 and 2 of the UN Universal Declaration of Human Rights:

1. All human beings are born free and equal in dignity and rights. They are endowed with reason and conscience and should act towards one another in a spirit of brotherhood.
2. Everyone is entitled to all the rights and freedoms set forth in this Declaration without distinction of any kind, such as race, colour, sex, language, religion, political or other opinion, national or social origin, property, birth or other status.

Article 2 follows Article 1, whereby the essential dignity of the person is the organizing principle informing international human rights. The sociologist Philip Hodgkiss has attempted to develop a wide-ranging schematic approach to the question of human dignity.[18] He has suggested three elements in a historic appreciation of dignity, all of which largely coexist today. First, considered as 'decorative', denoting rank, status and standing associated with questions of privilege and the depiction of private and public worth within society, as 'a touchstone of inequality'. Second, in terms of an intrinsic individual property suggesting personal character and esteem. Third, in a 'declarative' sense in terms of a universal ethical ideal inherent in humanity which can assume a defined legal or political status. Dignity is something to behold in the worth of others rather than something we feel, such as sympathy and compassion. He suggests dignity has become a key theme of contemporary life and dates its deployment in our secular lives from Enlightenment and the Romantic period due to the precarious status of human dignity under industrial capitalism; the dignity of our human labour. The origins of sociology captured this reality, Marx in his concerns with 'alienation', Durkheim with 'anomie' and Weber through the effects of industrial bureaucracy.

The dignity of labour can be understood in a decorative sense, that all types of jobs be respected equally, and no occupation considered superior in terms of awarding esteem and reward. Yet within Christian ethics and specifically Catholic Social Teaching, the dignity of labour stretches beyond this thin usage. *Rerum Novarum*, or *Rights and Duties of Capital and Labour*, issued by Pope Leo XIII on 15 May 1891,[19] remains an extraordinary condemnation of industrial capitalism and the immiseration of the working class. It asserts the moral imperative to regulate capitalism and established 'a preferential option for the poor' in the evolution of Catholic thought. This creed advocated unions, collective bargaining and a living wage to maintain and respect the dignity of the person in the workplace, created in the image of God. It urged the capitalist 'not to look upon their work-people as their bondsmen, but to respect in every man his dignity as a person ennobled of Christian character'.

Ninety years later, in *Laborem Exercens*, Pope John Paul II offered a restatement of 'personalism' within this tradition.[20] It begins by elaborating why work is not simply a commodity or random action but essential to human nature, 'a fundamental dimension of human existence on earth' and that 'man is the subject of work' and by acting on nature through work finds fulfilment and becomes 'more of a human being'. The text asserts that labour takes precedence over capital and the need for work protections to halt the violations of dignity, including unemployment, wage inequalities, job insecurities and technological change. The last of which can 'supplant' the person, 'taking away all personal satisfaction and the incentive to creativity and responsibility, when it deprives many workers of their previous employment, or when, through exalting the machine, it reduces man to the status of its slave'. Work is a spiritual activity, following in the footsteps of a carpenter, through which man collaborates 'for the redemption of humanity'. John Paul distinguishes between work and toil, the latter the product of sin, and although inseparable, the task is to nurture fulfilling work. The current Pope Francis remains a radical advocate of this intellectual inheritance, stating on Twitter in 2014: 'How I wish everyone had decent work! It is essential for human dignity'.

A recurring drumbeat within Catholic thought is the recognition of dignity in others as a means of recognizing it in ourselves, and transposing this universal religious signature into an appreciation of the capitalist employment relationship and the duties of employer and worker. A transhistorical spiritual belief in the dignity of the person is moulded into an understanding of how under certain social relations our common humanity can be violated and how work can affirm or degrade this abstract sentiment.

We can therefore identify three general 'declarative' traditions related to the universal ethical ideal of dignity and humanity, consequently shaping legal and political interventions under capitalism. These cover both religious traditions and secular humanist concerns at the consequences of mechanization and bureaucratization and the desire for autonomy and human self-actualization, together with human rights frameworks which often attempt to secularize Christian natural law traditions. All three approaches have influenced the character of the left and often have been allied in an ongoing contest with more utilitarian, economistic traditions. Such ethical and political themes have also been explored dramatically.

Talking Heads

Krzysztof Kieslowski died on 13 March 1996 aged 54. By then the Polish film director had established a worldwide reputation as a central figure in European cinema, best known for a series of films released in the years immediately before his death. These included the *Three Colours* trilogy (1993–4) and *The Double Life of Veronique* (1991), together with the *Dekalog* (1989), ten hour-long films originally created for Polish TV and shot on the same Warsaw apartment complex, loosely depicting the Ten Commandments.

Kieslowski's contribution to humanist film making stands as a critique of both the Polish communist regime and the corrupt materialism of the market society that followed. The political significance of his work is contested, not least because of a tendency to address moral concerns in the everyday lives of the characters rather than overtly political ones. For instance, whilst the 'three colours' express the French tricolour – 'blue' for liberty, 'white' for equality and 'red' for fraternity – the films themselves are rooted in practical ethical dilemmas that confront the characters rather than projecting clear political themes.

This concern with moral issues over straightforward political ones had been the evolving feature of his work. In his early career he was known for documentaries depicting the lives of Polish citizens. Later, as part of a group of film makers, he experimented with social realism and 'the cinema of moral anxiety'. This evolved into a series of feature films portraying the oppressive totalitarian character of Polish society culminating in 1981 with *Blind Chance*, made as the Solidarity movement grew and martial law was imposed. That same year, not by coincidence, a Polish Pope published *Laborem Exercens* on the dignity of human labour.

A short, overlooked film is the most powerful, and personal, in the auteur's catalogue. In revealing an essential humanism, he subtly reconciles his political and moral concerns. The fourteen-minute documentary *Gadające Głowy*, translated as *Talking Heads*, was released in 1980. It is a film documentary that is simple and straightforward yet in a few minutes confronts fundamental questions of moral and political philosophy. In it he asked a cross section of Polish citizens three simple questions: Who are you? Where do you come from? What is most important to you, what would you like from life? The film chronologically assembles the responses, starting with a newborn baby and closing with a woman aged 100, as their birth years are recorded on the screen, from 1979 to 1880. Each individual answers these basic questions of identity and the lives they wish to live or wish they had lived.

What is striking is the consistency of the responses, expressions of shared desires to live rewarding, good lives, for themselves and others. A transcendent story is established out of the mouths of strangers. The film documents how people wish to dwell, to live without anxiety amongst their personal landmarks. Consistent responses include a desire to be creative and more engaged with nature; a search for wisdom, courage and liberty. To live without fear and care for family and friends, an attachment to home and a belief in reason and duty, a desire for democratic change and resistance to nepotism and opportunism. A belief in kindness and the search for greater knowledge together with the desire for a clear conscience, honesty and justice. Good health, an end to suffering and humiliation. Hopes for children, grandchildren and wider humanity; peace, above all dignity, at times painfully expressed in grief and loss.

What quietly, beautifully emerges is the sense of a common life shared across ages and classes; a universal human life. It reveals an enduring idealism amongst people of all ages, from 'a realization that materialism isn't everything' to a consistent desire to be free, for peace and to live without fear. A recurring theme is self-identification through labour. Carers, teachers, labourers, assorted crafts people, intellectuals, amongst others, express a powerful sense of vocation, attached to wider desires such as freedom, democracy and security. The intergenerational belief in the dignity of the work itself, from labourer to intellectual, makes the labour appear indivisible. It echoes

Seamus Heaney's ownership of the vocations of bog cutter and poet in 'Digging'. Both establish historical continuity through a rendering of human dignity through labour.

It was filmed in 1979, the year that Margaret Thatcher came to power, and two years before Geoffrey Howe's infamous 1981 Budget, a landmark in British neo-liberalism. It was shot a year before the Solidarity union emerged in the Lenin shipyards and a decade before the collapse of the Eastern Bloc. Politics no longer asks the type of questions posed by Kieslowski. As the neo-liberal and social democratic traditions are beset by crisis and we are consumed by pandemic, it is a good time to ask them once more. If they speak to an essential humanism, the answers will be no different to those within Kieslowski's affirmative study, where strangers connect as a community. So, what do we know?

7

What Do We Think and What's Going to Happen?

What do we think about work? It dominates our life, structures our daily routines and generally informs what we do between leaving education and retiring. It helps shape not just how we subsist but what defines us – beyond self-worth, or personal standing, and the worth and standing of others – but a deeper shared humanity. So, what do we know?

In their 1972 book *The Hidden Injuries of Class*, Richard Sennett and Jonathan Cobb explored the significance of work in people's lives, beyond subsistence and material success, in terms of what people value, their confusions and sense of alienation.[1] What happens when we are unable to live the lives we wish? How, given the myth of meritocracy, do we understand the personal shame and humiliation that work can bring? Specifically, they addressed the divide between what we wish and what we experience in terms of the labour we perform and how this finds expression in painful feelings of self-worth, indeed self-loathing, even when we succeed materially.

Twenty-five years later Sennett returned to these themes in *The Corrosion of Character* and found significant changes in modern work in terms of discretion, isolation, lack of advancement and progression, greater flexibility and contingency within the new economy.[2] He concluded that the modern world of work is corroding our character in terms of our long-term emotional experiences, personal fidelities and attachments, both to people and organizations. He ends with the suggestion that a system 'which provides human beings no deep reasons to care about one another cannot long preserve its legitimacy'. Leading academics, such as Sandel and Sennett, regularly return to the character of modern work to address wider challenges in how we live together and the resilience of our liberal democracies.

Throughout his career Sennett has studied how people embed within communities and the stable attachments provided by work and craft, how they help nurture mutual obligations and shared respect through ritual and civility. Yet he argues this is dwindling in the new economy where isolation and a growing precariat undermine these cohesive possibilities. These themes align with the work of thinkers such as Zygmunt Bauman when identifying the significance of insecure work in shaping our wider sense of self, such as his diagnosis of 'liquid life' that explores the consequences of the faster, more turbulent lives we are forced to live.[3] For writers such as Sennett and Bauman, contemporary life is marked by transience and insecure and inconsequential existence, diminishing what was once solid in our lives through increased market competition. People are treated less as emotionally literate beings, more as consumers or degraded units of labour. Our lives are in flux. What was once secure is now temporary, driven by a changing labour market and creating a heightened sense of national insecurity. This comes at great cost and undermines our personal wellbeing as our existence is privatized. Their contributions echo the famous Berger and Neuhaus thesis from 1977 that significant 'mediating structures', such as that of family, church, workplace and neighbourhood, enable people to live enhanced lives and that the decline in such structures, or landmarks, comes with significant consequences in terms of our sense of community and attachment.[4]

Does the empirical research into attitudes to work back up such a negative diagnosis? If such epic transformations define late capitalism, there should be ample research to support such claims. The data suggest a more complicated picture, however. Research tends to support the basic observation that we hold contradictory, paradoxical feelings about work and, even before the disruptive effects of pandemic, points to recent heightened concerns about the work we perform amongst a significant minority of our fellow citizens. However, it suggests significant differences in the experience and attitudes towards unrewarding work.

At a basic level evidence tells us work remains a significant landmark in our lives. British Social Attitudes data suggest overall levels of job satisfaction in 2015 were similar to a decade earlier with 15 per cent 'completely satisfied', 27 per cent 'very satisfied' and 38 per cent 'fairly satisfied' with their work. A majority responded that they would enjoy working even if they didn't need the money, suggesting intrinsic value attached to work beyond material reward. This appears to have been slowly increasing over time, although responses vary depending on class and education. Professional or managerial responses and from graduates were more positive compared to those in routine or semi-routine occupations or those with no qualifications. Overall, only 13 per cent rated having a high income as 'very important'.[5]

Separately the polling company YouGov put a dilemma to the public: would you rather have a job you hate that pays well, or a job you love that pays poorly? The public overwhelmingly plumped for passion over pay, with approaching two-thirds saying they'd rather have a poorly paid job they loved compared to just 18 per cent who'd prefer a well-paid job they hated.[6]

The British Social Attitudes data tell us 92 per cent of respondents rank job security as important and 90 per cent rate having an interesting job highly. Good opportunities for advancement and a job that was helpful to others and/ or useful to society are also particularly important. Here degrees of separation between what we want and what we experience begin to emerge. Only two-thirds of workers believe they have appropriate job security, this percentage having fallen amongst the lower social classes and older workers. In 2015, 37 per cent found their work stressful either 'always' or 'often' compared to 28 per cent in 1989, suggesting significant work intensification.

For over thirty years these surveys have measured job quality using seven characteristics: job security, high incomes, opportunities for advancement, whether jobs help people, whether they are useful to society, whether they are interesting, and whether they allow for independence. They reveal a stark segmentation of attitudes. The overall proportion they identify as holding a good job has increased, from 57 per cent in 1989 to 71 per cent in 2015. The lower social classes are much less likely to have a job with four or more positive attributes than their counterparts in higher social classes. These findings are backed up by other data suggesting people search for security through their work[7] yet are registering heightened insecurity about their jobs and futures.[8]

Similar patterns were reported by Ipsos MORI in research for the Fabian Society on changing work attitudes since the millennium.[9] Most people hold positive views about their work: 79 per cent agree that their work is interesting, 78 per cent find it enjoyable and 63 per cent always look forward to work or do so most of the time. Ten per cent of workers disagree that their work is enjoyable, 11 per cent don't find it interesting, and 12 per cent always or regularly wish they didn't have to go to work. Working-class respondents find their work significantly less interesting and enjoyable, just over half looking forward to going to work, compared to 66 per cent of white-collar workers.

The polling suggested key drivers of unenjoyable work: lack of flexibility, agency, initiative and security. The Fabian Society concluded that emerging work narratives of an employment crisis or a workless future, or government assumptions that all work is good and fulfilling, fail to reflect the opinions of workers. Such narratives lack complexity and nuance. Millions of people have positive experiences at work every day, but significant segments of the labour market do not.

People appear generally satisfied with their work, yet evidence implies a growing labour market minority where insecurity drives more negative attitudes. A study by the Institute for Public Policy Research (IPPR) suggests today's generation of younger workers risk losing out on access to permanent, secure and fulfilling work compared to previous generations, as they are more likely to be in work characterized by contractual flexibility, including part-time or temporary work and self-employment.[10] They are also more likely to be underemployed and/or overqualified. Consequently, they are more likely to experience poorer mental health and wellbeing linked to experiencing labour market insecurities.

The New Economics Foundation suggests secure, well-paid work is a key marker of national success,[11] yet reference Labour Force Survey (LFS) data to identify those defined to be in 'good jobs' to have proportionally decreased whilst employment rose between 2011 and 2014. They argue many of the recently created jobs to be either low-paid, insecure, or both, leaving nearly a third of the labour force either without work, or without good work. The TUC 'Insecure Work' report estimates 3.7 million people experiencing insecurity at work.[12] They reference the Resolution Foundation use of LFS data to suggest that whilst the level of workforce insecurity has not changed much in the last two decades, it has significantly increased since the recession in certain types of atypical and low-quality employment, including involuntary part-time working, insecure self-employment and zero-hours contracts. Each affects a relatively small number of employees yet taken together they imply a sizeable minority who face acute forms of job insecurity, influencing their attitudes to work.

A wealth of evidence points to job quality having an important bearing on health. Research suggests a declining sense of wellbeing due to being made unemployed, and that the economically inactive experience worse mental health than those in work. Yet people employed in low-paying or highly stressful jobs may not actually enjoy better health than those who remain unemployed.[13] A paid job is by no means a guarantee of wellbeing. The quality of employment is known to impact on people's health, life expectancy and life chances. Jobs associated with better health and wellbeing are generally those with greater variety, autonomy, security and better workplace relationships as well as financial rewards.[14]

For a significant, growing section of the labour force, work wellbeing is being reduced. Insecure jobs with low status and high levels of strain can damage mental and physical health. Reviewing the data, the Resolution Foundation concluded the most important intergenerational issue for the government to address should be job stability and security.[15]

An unequal virus plays directly into this emerging picture of segmentation and work insecurity linked to questions of age, sector and geography. Whilst transforming many things, the pandemic has also consolidated these labour market trends. Under-25s have been hardest hit by the Covid-19 economic fallout. Younger and older workers were the most likely to have lost their jobs or had their incomes reduced. In the first month of the lockdown alone, one in three young people were furloughed or lost their jobs, and over one in three had their pay reduced since the crisis started. This was accounted for by the large number of young people employed in the sectors most severely affected by the lockdown, such as leisure, retail and hospitality.

In terms of fairness at work, recent data conclude a majority of employees thought their organization treated people fairly, although only a quarter strongly held this view. Two out of ten did not consider their organizations fair. High levels of perceived fairness were associated with greater work motivations, commitment to the organization and willingness to put in discretionary effort. Pay relativities were only weakly related to perceived fairness, but job quality and social relations in the enterprise were strongly associated, especially the control people could exercise over their work tasks, the helpfulness of supervisors, opportunities to participate in organizational decisions and job security.

Fairness at work is central to employee wellbeing, affecting both psychological and physical health risks. This is true in terms of both procedural fairness and insecurity and norms of reciprocity, the balance between 'effort and reward'. There is a strong association between perceived fairness and a range of indicators of job performance, organizational commitment and wellbeing at work. The two factors that most strongly undermine a sense of fairness are high levels of work intensity and job insecurity.[16]

Overall, the research suggests a segmented labour market with segmented attitudes driven by levels of insecurity and work quality expressed demographically by age and class. We can conclude that secure work that offers autonomy can help citizens flourish. People search for dignity through their work. Workers receive respect and gain status from others for the job they do. Work can demonstrate citizenship and standing through a productive contribution to a wider sense of community.

People desire appropriate income from their work, although they tend not instrumentalize work and value the freedom that work offers. Human autonomy and freedom from fear and domination are important in our work relations and remain a source of creativity and self-control in our wider lives.[17]

People desire good work; it provides our primary source of income and shapes our identities and communities. Conversely, insecure work can flatten esteem and can constrain opportunities to flourish. Seen in these terms a celebration of a world without work appears simplistic and as one-sided as the treasury economist churning out labour market aggregates to indicate national success.

Over 25 years ago Will Hutton suggested Britain had developed a fractured '30/30/40' society – 30 per cent disadvantaged and marginalized, 30 per cent insecure, 40 per cent privileged.[18] Modern capitalism, preoccupied with short-term gain rather than building businesses and husbanding workforces, had built a precarious system dependent on indentured consumption. Surveying the data and following a financial crash and a pandemic, this description appears relevant still today. Yet people's desires have not changed in terms of their attachment to secure, rewarding work. Their chances of securing such work were declining, however, even before the disastrous labour market consequences of the pandemic. These most recent effects have tended to reinforce a trend towards a deeply segmented labour market, and without a sustained political pushback could well validate the earlier insights of writers such as Bauman and Sennett in their negative assessment of work futures, at least for a significant section of society. All the data reinforce the requirement for political action, consolidated by the experiences of pandemic. Yet politicians don't know where to turn.

We concluded the first part of the book with the most recent Skills and Employment Survey study of productivity drivers in the economy. These tend to reinforce an analysis of segmented labour market trends and work intensification accounting for sluggish growth. The drivers of productivity also appear to correspond to what people desire in their work: autonomy, influence and discretion over their labour, voice, responsive management, the prevalence of initiative taking, innovation, high-impact suggestion making and high-productivity-enhancing jobs. Since 2006 these productivity drivers have all become less prevalent and productivity has at best flatlined.[19]

The work characteristics driving productivity correspond to many we might identify in good dignified work and further correspond to what people want from their labour. On all three fronts – even before the pandemic struck – we were heading in the wrong direction in terms of productivity shortfalls, declining work quality and growing pessimism about our working lives. The pandemic appears to have further consolidated these trends and requires a new political response. Yet many persist in assuming technology will soon render such findings and feelings obsolete.

'Technology Is not Destiny'

The robots are coming. Work is ending, or at least being fundamentally transformed. We will witness the wholesale replacement of humans by machines. Given what we know about how we value work, these are clutch calls in our future wellbeing. So, what do we really know about work futures?

Assertions of 'technological disruption' have always been around. Keynes argued that by 2030 the average working week would be 15 hours as new methods of economizing on labour exceed its new uses.[20]

As noted in the Prologue, headlines on work futures often derive from a single, contested source. Osborne and Frey in 2013 estimated that up to half of British jobs were threatened by automation – famously used two years later by the Bank of England to assert 15 million UK jobs to be at risk.[21] Countless headlines followed.

Yet wildly different estimates exist. McKinsey Global suggest only 5 per cent of jobs are candidates for full automation.[22] PWC estimate up to 30 per cent of British jobs are at high risk by the 2030s.[23] Yet it is the Oxford study and Bank estimates that dominate.

While not conclusive, the evidence tends to suggest the risk of automation is greatest to occupations and tasks in low-skill, low-pay sectors: transport and storage, retail and administration and support services. Over 15 per cent of the UK workforce is employed in retail, broadly defined to include logistics, sales, packaging and distribution. In the UK, workers in low-skill occupations account for 45 per cent of the UK labour market, or 13.9 million workers, with significant regional variations.

This is not one-way traffic, however, even though Frey and Osborne do not consider new jobs created by automation. Technology will have diverse impacts across sectors. Growth can be expected in sectors such as health and social care, the creative industries and leisure, in sectors that require interpersonal, human-centred and creative skills, as well as in the technology and telecommunications sector working on AI, data analytics, fintech and biotech. The service sector is likely to be the major driver of employment growth – it already accounts for about 80 per cent of GDP in the UK.

Alarmingly, many of these studies often don't even contain timelines. For instance, McKinsey, based on an analysis of 800 occupations, estimate half of all work activities taking place today could be automated by 2055, although this could 'happen 20 years earlier or later'. So, what is rigorous estimation, what is speculation?

Other studies suggest Frey and Osborne are methodologically flawed in that they overestimate job automatability; many jobs are very hard to automate. Moreover, changes due to technology often alter certain tasks within occupations rather than whole occupations. Even where a job can in a technical case be automated, it might not be cost-effective. It might be simply cheaper to employ human beings. Many of these studies underplay any appreciation of patterns of labour regulation that help or hinder automation. Take the classic example, the resurgence of hand carwashes and the untimely disappearance of the apparently more advanced automated alternative, supported by the illegal exploitation of migrant labour in the deregulated British labour market.[24]

Back to the statistics. The Organisation for Economic Co-operation and Development (OECD) estimate on average, for the 21 OECD countries, 9 per cent of jobs are automatable.[25] They also suggest this is an overestimate given likely political and social constraints, redeployment and future job generation and conclude, 'Automation and digitalization are unlikely to destroy large numbers of jobs'. Others also urge caution as it is not easy to automate human dexterity and common sense.[26] A TUC discussion paper, drawing on Frey and Osborne, the Bank and PWC calculations, estimate between 10 and 30 per cent of UK jobs to be at risk yet conclude 'The likelihood is that these jobs could be replaced by new occupations and professions'.[27]

The evidence appears at best inconclusive. Certainly, the UK government does not appear to be excessively worried. Their 'Industrial Strategy' White Paper suggests an optimistic future and a growing demand for high-skilled workers, anticipating an extra 1.8 million new jobs in the next ten years.[28] The government continues to focus on questions of supply rather than anticipate a collapse in the demand for labour.

In a thorough review of the literature Philip Brown and colleagues from Cardiff University conclude that 'technology is not destiny' and that human decisions will determine the future of work:

> Blanket claims about the impact of digital technologies overlook the way that they are applied across sectors and occupations. Typically, it is low-skilled jobs that are assumed to be most in danger. However, there is growing evidence of new technologies transforming professional, managerial and technical occupations. Moreover, the studies reviewed rarely consider the potential for job creation around automation, or for the relocation of those made redundant as a result of automation.
>
> Most studies focus on the potential for automation, without incorporating into their models economic and social factors that may stimulate or deter the replacement of workers by technology (i.e. politics). As such, much of the literature falls back on technological determinism, with little reference to the way companies 'choose' to deploy new technologies or to the capitalist economy, which is the engine for technological innovation.[29]

Their study is highly critical of three general approaches to future labour demand and skills formation through technological change. First, the largely optimistic account of future knowledge work developed by human capital analysts and skill-biased technological change theorists. Second, the more pessimistic view of deskilling and routinization, not just due to technological innovation but also to the imperatives of capitalism, leading some to suggest a modern 'digital Taylorism', echoing Braverman's earlier analysis of the degradation of work and mechanical Taylorism. Some writers have also pointed to the ways in which digital technologies have been used to develop flexible labour, in insecure or precarious jobs.[30] Third, the automation-led 'end-of-work' thesis pioneered by writers such as Jeremy Rifkin, André Gorz and Paul Mason, which suggests that work is ending and offers new possibilities for enduring human liberation and future abundance rather than scarcity.[31] They find the various automation literatures unpersuasive, not just empirically but theoretically, due to their incipient technological determinism. The robots might not be marching after all.

So the future appears far from certain. It depends on the policy and political choices we make. In recent years UK labour markets have seen a significant increase in non-standard employment contracts and atypical work, including elements of the 'gig economy'. There are now 5 million self-employed workers, a million workers on zero-hours contracts, and 800,000 agency workers in the UK, since 2008 rises of 24, 450 and 46 per cent, respectively. These comparatively high numbers are the product of our labour law and policy choices rather than simply being technologically determined, resulting in work that is more 'divisible', less regulated and protected, and which contributes to sluggish wage growth.[32]

Again, it is worth concluding with *The Skills and Employment Survey 2017*, the seventh in a series which began in 1986, which provides the most up-to-date picture of skills and attitudes to work. Its authors suggest a 'picture of a stagnating or even reversing demand for skills' since 2012. Until 2012, the share of graduate-level jobs in the workforce expanded steadily by around three percentage points every five years since the series began in 1986. Over the same period, the fraction of jobs that require no formal qualifications diminished. Since 2012, however, these proportions have not changed significantly. The data on technical change suggests workers in more skilled positions experience a greater incidence of technical change. Yet the incidence of technical change has been *falling continuously since 2001 in high-skilled occupations* and *since 2006 across all occupation groups.*[33]

There is little consensus about future disruption; the research is contested and is at best unclear. It is often speculative and contains serious methodological flaws. The lack of compelling evidence suggests a more cautious approach with an emphasis on our political choices rather than reverting to conjecture fuelled by technological determinism. It has always been the case. Pre-war Dagenham revealed how technological change enabled the mass production of goods, using assembly lines and interchangeable labour processes – mechanical Taylorism. Yet it was an ongoing political contest with obvious relevance today with suggestions of modern communications technology propelling new forms of digital Taylorism alongside a general growth in precarious forms of labour. There is nothing inevitable here; it is contested political terrain because of the nature of human labour that defines the political character of its regulation under capitalism. It means we need to return to politics.

8
Justice and the Left

Three Speeches

Just over fifty years ago, on 18 March 1968, Bobby Kennedy gave a speech at the University of Kansas,[1] where he suggested:

> Even if we act to erase material poverty, there is another great task, it is to confront the poverty of satisfaction – purpose and dignity – that afflicts us all.

He went further in separating ethics from economics:

> The gross national product does not allow for the health of our children, the quality of their education or the joy of their play. It does not include the beauty of our poetry or the strength of our marriages, the intelligence of our public debate or the integrity of our public officials.
>
> It measures neither our wit nor our courage, neither our wisdom nor our learning, neither our compassion nor our devotion to our country, *it measures everything in short, except that which makes life worthwhile.*

The speech, with its emphasis on spiritual fulfilment and the search for meaning and dignity rather than unbridled growth, echoed themes developed four years earlier when Lyndon Johnson spoke of an 'opportunity to move not only toward the rich society and the powerful society, but upward to the Great Society'.[2] Material justice was not enough. He talked of 'the desire for beauty and the hunger for community', where 'the meaning of our lives matches the marvelous products of our labor'. He recited Aristotle and identified the city, country and classroom where this Great Society was to be created in order to move beyond a 'soulless wealth'. The task being to 'help build a society where the demands of morality, and the needs of the spirit, can be realized in the life of the Nation'.

Both speeches predate 'neo-liberalism' and contain a language unrecognizable on the left today. It is, however, one recognizable within the history of the left, in the ethical concerns of Labour leaders such as Lansbury, Hardie and MacDonald, labelled the 'apostles of the old faith' by the great Labour historian Ken Morgan. Such passions inspired a young Clem Attlee to sidestep the Fabians and help form the Stepney Independent Labour Party (the ILP) in 1912. A similar cadence reappeared in elements of New Left humanism reacting against the Stalinism of the late 1950s. Yet today we are more likely to hear this type of political language on the right rather than the left.

In Indianapolis, on 22 July 1999, George W. Bush gave a speech entitled 'The Duty of Hope'.[3] Notionally a short, simple speech, it sought to forge a new centre-right public philosophy. It began with an acknowledgement that the invisible hand 'cannot touch the human heart'. From there on three words dominate – duty, hope, compassion – blending a patriotism 'tied together by bonds of friendship, and community and solidarity'.

Bush argued that the 'government' must act in the common good – and that good is not common until it is shared by those in need'. Marvin Olasky cites this speech as the key text in his account of the origins of modern

'Compassionate Conservatism'. Its reach spread across the Atlantic, informing the modernization of the Tories under Cameron.

The speech speaks to idealism, romanticism and hope – routed through both a national, patriotic story and a local parochial one; a method consistently used in the way Bush referenced local initiatives through allegory to tell deeper national stories 'rich in justice and compassion and family love and moral outrage'. It creates grip and visceral power – and political energy – because of this capacity to anchor abstract philosophical propositions in everyday stories to establish a political sentiment.

'Compassionate Conservatism' was a conscious political project to push back against a soulless and destructive economic liberalism that threatened conservatism. Its ambition was to reach beyond liberal economic calculus and return the conservative political tradition to questions of justice and ethics. This brief, failed movement sought to recapture conservatism from the economic purists by colonizing a language once associated with civil rights and the US Democrats. It did not last – neither did talk of the 'Big Society' in the UK. In 2012, identifying tensions across the Republican right, before the Trump appropriation, US columnist David Brookes wrote that 'economic conservatives have taken control. Traditional conservatism has gone into eclipse'.[4]

All three speeches talk of love, hope and duty; of patriotism, family and religion. All use notions of 'community' and the 'common life'. Their aim is a renewed political sentiment to contest nationhood anchored in ethics rather than economics. A similar language, texture and method are contained within each speech. They are all built around the notion of virtue, specifically the cardinal virtue compassion, within either a secularized Christian ethical frame, or in the case of Bush an explicit religious call to arms, and all cohere around a notion of reciprocity and the idea of the 'common good'.

Historically in this country reciprocity was the ethical

core of the left – the give and take that creates the social bonds that hold people together in a common life. It was not exclusively religious. Whilst it is the hallmark of Christian Socialism, it also established William Morris's notion of fellowship. These speeches suggest a lost language in a political world dominated by questions of utility. That is because they operate within an alternative framework of justice unfashionable in politics today.

Politics, Morality and Justice

Kieslowski's short, simple film *Talking Heads* reveals ordinary people's hopes and desires and suggests a human personality removed from our public conversation. This sense of a lost political vocabulary is corroborated by the three American speeches. All four operate within a tradition of justice outside mainstream political and philosophical debate and reveal something politics has lost.[5]

Political debate, both *within and between parties and traditions*, is grounded within alternative philosophical approaches to questions of justice. Kieslowski's *Three Colours* triptych not only expressed the tricolour, 'white' for equality, 'blue' for liberty and 'red' for fraternity, but also three competing philosophical traditions concerned with maximizing either *human welfare, freedom* or *virtue*.[6] The first tends to consider the material wellbeing of the people as the measure of justice; the second is concerned with a respect for, and the extension of, personal rights and freedoms; the third the promotion of virtue. It is within this third tradition that Kieslowski's film and the contribution of the three Americans can be situated. The film is especially compelling because it is ordinary people – rather than politicians or academics – that speak a language rarely heard. The moral significance of work, the dignity of labour, has always been a central political concern within this tradition. As the standing of this tradition has declined so has political concern for the dignity of labour.

Welfare

Welfare models of justice rely on utilitarian philosophical assumptions and interventions which seek to maximize the happiness of the maximum number of people. This is generally translated to mean their material wellbeing, their welfare. They tend to be interested primarily in the efficient allocation of economic resources. Within the UK social democratic left, it is often associated with the work of the Fabian Society and a generation of economists and planners that took hold of the top strata of the Labour Party throughout the 1930s under the sponsorship of the great economist, politician and eventual Chancellor Hugh Dalton. It is regularly described as 'labourist', a term which has come to mean modest economic reform and minor redistribution executed by a central Labour government aided by strong institutional trade union support.

Questions of power and democracy tend to be neglected within this tradition – it is often described as 'economistic' or economically 'deterministic'. This approach, especially on the left, tends to envision the task of politics as one of state capture to redistribute and maximize the welfare of the people. As such, it tends to be criticized for technocratic forms of social administration and for a centralizing, bureaucratic statecraft – a tendency towards 'statism'.

This economistic or distributional tradition continues to dominate contemporary left thinking. A good recent example is the ex-Labour leader Ed Miliband's 'cost of living' framework, which was heavily defeated at the 2015 General Election. The policy strategy was one of money transfers – such as capping energy prices and rents, abolition of the bedroom tax, higher minimum wages and capping student fees – essentially fiscal exchanges administered by a central bureaucracy. Under New Labour, as discussed in chapter 4, the distributional approach especially favoured by Miliband's mentor Gordon Brown was of remedial money transfers – tax credits – to buttress the disposable incomes of workers as wages flatlined due to global competitive pressures, funded by growth engineered through a compact with finance capital. This tradition has dominated the history of Labour since the 1930s.

Such an approach has also defined Marxism with assumptions of the domination of the economic 'base' over 'superstructure' and of the forces over the relations of production driving towards the overall wellbeing of the masses. Once again, the charge is 'economic reductionism' or 'technological determinism' and associated tendencies to downgrade questions of democracy and power as humans tend to be considered simple carriers of these economic laws – bearers of modes of production. Its Ricardian heritage also privileges a politics of distribution over one of work very much alive today with talk of accelerationism, postcapitalism and post-workerism. Across both the left and right wings of Labour, utilitarian thinking continues to dominate; various factional warriors have more in common than they realize.

Freedom

In contrast to questions of utility, an alternative tradition has focused on questions of freedom and rights. On the political right we can situate the free market libertarians. Neo-liberalism is best understood as a combination of the utility theory of Neo-Classical Economics and philosophical concerns with liberty. On the left are those who seek to establish human rights that remedy economic and social disadvantage. This is often described as the preserve of the 'liberal left', leading some to question if it constitutes part of 'the left' at all. Marx, for example, mocked the 'so-called rights of man' and it is an approach widely abused by the reductive economistic left.

However, questions of democracy and liberty have a proud left-wing heritage informing, amongst others, eighteenth-century Radical Liberalism, the Levellers, Tom Paine and Chartism. More recently, the consequence of industrial society and experiences of twentieth-century fascist and Stalinist authoritarian regimes have elevated this tradition across the left to protect an essential human dignity. The post-war Universal Declaration of Human Rights, for instance, was guided by both Enlightenment and modern social democratic and socialist rights-based thinking. In the UK pioneering social reforms of the 1960s under the guidance of Roy Jenkins revealed its influence within Labour, as did, decades later, initiatives such as the Human Rights Act under the Blair government.

Philosophically, this approach was given extra intellectual support and energy by the political philosopher John Rawls and his groundbreaking 1971 book *A Theory of Justice*.[7] His conception of the modern social contract re-established for the left the notion of liberty whilst permitting economic inequality – but only so long as it benefited the least well off. More generally, the rights approach seeks a non-judgemental state architecture, which cultivates the ability of each and every citizen to choose the way they wish to live their lives and actively equips them with the ability to do so; as such it retains a liberal neutrality on what constitutes the good life – that is for each and every citizen to decide.

Virtue

The third approach is more ethical in orientation and more ancient. It is concerned with nurturing the human characteristics upon which a good or just society is formed. It suggests a more judgemental framework than others that rest on questions of utility or rights. Aristotle remains the classical reference point regarding the virtues that should be nurtured in the public space and the policy and institutional arrangements that enable citizens to live a good life.

This approach has been generally exiled from modern thinking, especially on the left. Yet it maintains a rich history within English socialism and lies deep within parts of the Labour Party and a wider ethical Christian and secularized left.

Virtue politics tends to be seen – especially in the United States – as the preserve of cultural conservatives and the religious right. Yet much civil rights thinking drew on moral and religious concerns rather than from liberalism and has consistently informed part of the democratic US left tradition. The speeches of Kennedy, Johnson and Bush speak to various streams within this tradition. As a 2008 candidate, the Obama language of moral seriousness stood outside the confines of liberal managerialism, although once in office he did very little to confront Wall Street following the financial crash.

The field of virtue ethics concentrates on the classic ideals such as honour, duty, justice, wisdom and fortitude to evaluate the reasoning behind moral decision making – as opposed to a mere adherence to rules or the outcome of the action. Aristotle's concern was human flourishing – the practices that help cultivate good character and habits and the state of human life that could only be properly achieved in the city-state community.

The notion of the common good associated with this tradition is concerned with personal and mutual flourishing in terms of our talents and vocations, treating people as belonging to families, localities and communities and to shared traditions, interests and faiths neglected by an exclusively legalistic, managerial and technocratic conception of justice and politics.

The guiding philosophy of the common good is the mutual recognition that we are each dependent upon other people throughout our lives, and that we need one another to succeed individually. In industrial society, the call of solidarity upheld this interdependency especially in terms of the dignity of labour. It did so by appealing to an underlying, common identity that echoes our earlier discussion of an essential 'declarative' human dignity. As politics has become increasingly instrumental and economistic, it helps retrieve a language around what it is to live a good life. Both neo-liberal globalization and the modern utilitarianism detach economic and political power from locality, tradition and interpersonal relationships

The aspiration to lead a meaningful life goes deep into our modern consciousness. The desire is individual, but it is not selfish. For Charles Taylor it involves the right of everyone to achieve their own unique way of being human. To dispute this right in others is to fail to live within its own terms.[8] Our social bonds are realized in the ethic of reciprocity – do not do to others what you would not have them do to you. Our freedom is conditional upon the constraints of our obligation to others. Equality is not the imposition of sameness, nor the standardizing of our individuality: it is the ethical core of justice. It holds that each individual is irreplaceable, and it is the necessary condition for social freedom. It is an ideal in which freedom finds a synthesis with equality in an expression of our common humanity. Equality is bigger than distributive justice.

This justice schema helps us interpret impenetrable divisions and factions on the left and competing visions of socialism.

Rethinking Socialism

Socialist history often begins in 1848 with the publication of *The Communist Manifesto*,[9] although this inference of a Marxist year zero immediately disregards the contributions of figures like Gerrard Winstanley and the True Levellers or Diggers in their resistance to enclosure, or that of early nineteenth-century French and English Utopian Socialists such as Fourier and Owen. The 1848 departure point is at the expense of earlier ethical socialist movements.

Crosland's *The Future of Socialism* is another famous template to interrogate socialism.[10] He provided a grid of assorted 'socialisms' yet dodged a definition himself, suggesting it was about a 'strong' rather than 'liberal' equality. He emphasized the means beyond ownership to address freedom and democracy, planning and growth. His book is a brilliant blend of distributive, utilitarian economics and rights-based radical thinking. He identified twelve socialist doctrines that existed before his own. Three cover the value theories of Mill, Ricardo and Marx as well as a Fabian tradition, a Soviet-inspired 'planning' framework and a 'welfarist' or 'paternalist' approach. He also highlighted an early nineteenth-century 'natural law' doctrine of common land and a syndicalist or 'guild' tradition of industrial democracy. He added 'Owenism' – a utilitarian approach to economic cooperation before concluding with an ethical Christian Socialist tradition, an ILP doctrine of fellowship and the separate one of William Morris. A rather cumbersome dozen socialisms to add to his own.

R.H. Tawney defined socialism as resistance to the market and constraints to private profit.[11] He identified two general approaches to socialism: economic and ethical. The economic route is driven by socialized ownership to produce alterative allocations of resources to redress poverty, homelessness and the like. Here socialism is about resource distribution and utilitarian welfare maximization. The ethical approach is concerned with fellowship to contest the indignities of commodification and human dispossession, an approach to justice built around virtue.

This essential division within socialism does not depict a historic arc, such as a transition from Romanticism to modernism. Rather, it suggests a general philosophical fault line within the left; often expressed between scientific rationality and humanism, economism and ethics, stretching back to the seventeenth century. It stands as an ever-present division.

This divide between ethics and economic utility is one deployed by Ken Morgan in his attempts to delineate the early history of the Labour Party.[12] He considers the competing philosophies and practices of the 'ILP' and the 'Fabian' traditions, established in 1883 and 1884 respectively, as the best method to interpret labour history. The former is concerned primarily with questions of virtue, the latter with economic welfare. The virtue/welfare or ILP/Fabian divide helps us understand the politics of Labour from the late nineteenth century to the mid-1950s. From then on, we should add a third, rights-based approach to socialist justice. Although predating both 1883 and 1848, especially in the thinking of Paine and Chartism, this informs an appreciation of Labour politics following Crosland's 1956 masterwork and the influence of Rawlsian progressive thinking from the 1970s. This three-part schema moves us beyond the traditional left/right metric within the left. Not least because different factions often share very similar approaches to questions of justice.

A Different Marxism

The division between utility and virtue, economics and ethics, has also shaped the history of Marxism. On one side stands the historical materialism of the Second International which emphasized the naturalistic development of the laws of history and underplayed human action. On the other, humanist reactions which sought to put people back into history to contest scientific socialism and the realities of rigid party domination and a bureaucratized, authoritarian politics. This reoriented Marxism towards questions of ethics and virtue, aided by the discovery of some of the writings of the young Marx, most notably *The 1844 Manuscripts*.[13] This early emphasis on the normative components of human action later reappeared in the work of the original advocates of Critical Theory.[14]

A different response to the determinism of the Second International was offered by Structuralism within European Marxism. In contrast to the humanist reorientation, it sought to re-establish the scientific status of the Marxist project. This was dependent on clarifying the method by which Marx considered human agents as being 'decentred'; eliminating humans from the centre of social thought and instead providing a science of the structures, or levels, of social activity – the economic, political and ideological.

Although aimed at a 'Continental' Marxism, the critique of Althusser by E.P. Thompson is a fundamental reference in the evolution of a unique English socialist tradition. For Thompson, many of the central problems contained within structuralism could be resolved by *rejecting any attempt at establishing the scientific status of Marxist theory*. In contrast, he emphasized a tradition of open empirical inquiry within the work of Marx prior to his engagement with political economy which, he argued, formed the basis of historical materialism, seen as the contribution to a broad-ranging 'unitary knowledge of society'. For Thompson, attempts at establishing the scientific basis of Marxist thought produced a strictly enclosed conception of what constitutes knowledge; denying the importance of the subjective human condition and opening the door to a totalitarian politics.[15]

This signals a key divide within ethical traditions on the left, between humanist and religious approaches that follows a similar path to our earlier discussion of dignity. After the Second World War, from outside the Labour Party, elements of the so-called 'New Left' sought to focus on William Morris as part of a quest to rediscover a unique English socialist politics: one that owed a profound debt to English Romanticism, anti-scientific and artistic in orientation. This renewed emphasis on human dignity and creativity in its rejection of industrial capitalism was primarily to save Marxism – and Communism – from itself rather than any feelings for man created in the image of God, yet aligned with long-standing religious concerns across the left.

E.P. Thompson's work was part of a distinct political project within the Communist Party to identify a unique English radicalism – a politics of virtue – in the character of Morris, but also within the emerging working class itself.[16] Alongside Thompson, Raymond Williams, particularly in *Culture and Society*,[17] defined a political,

artistic and cultural tradition from John Ruskin, through
Morris, to the modern New Left. Ruskin helped shape this
tradition by his resistance to laissez-faire society and an
artistic criticism that asserted 'the art of any country is the
exponent of its social and political virtues . . . the exponent
of its ethical life'.[18] In contrast to the method of orthodox
economics and utilitarianism, value, in terms of what we
value in life, is taken out of the realm of technical political
economy – of supply and demand – and instead relates to
the virtue of the labour itself – seen as the 'joyful and right
exertion of perfect life in man'.[19]

Within the work of the religious Ruskin, the notion
of wealth and value, and indeed labour, is used to attack
nineteenth-century liberalism for its cold utilitarianism,
and promote a society governed by 'what kinds of labour
is good for men [sic], raising them and making them
happy', and challenge the human degradation intrinsic to
the emerging economic system.[20] This method within a
Romantic tradition, including both the religious and secular, foreshadowed Thompson's work on the formation
of the English working class, especially its early eighteenth-century radicalism and the effects of the Industrial
Revolution in establishing forms of mechanistic thought.
Such an approach – a thread from Ruskin through Morris
to the later concerns of the New Left – sought to retrieve
an approach to labour and value missing from forms of
political economy primarily concerned with price and
distribution.

Raymond Williams focused on this specific point
in *Culture and Society* in his discussion of how Morris
rejected the reformulation of value as 'exchange value'
contained in both orthodox Marxist and liberal economics. His conception of value inherited from Ruskin was
qualitatively distinct from any theory of embodied labour
times or of subjective preferences. Consequently, it offered
the potential of breaking through such a price-orientated
approach to human activity. It remains the source of a dis-
tinctly English, radical challenge to assorted economistic

socialisms driven by a concern for human creativity and self-realization through reimagining the intrinsic dignity of human labour. Morris is the critical link. His unique contribution ensured this tradition within socialist thought was attached to the political formation of an emerging nineteenth-century working class in the formation of the ILP and was retained well into the 1930s amongst later influential strands of the Labour Party.

The socialism of Morris was conceived in this emancipatory interpretation of human labour and its creative capacities. Art represents a politics of resistance to life being commodified through dispossession. As his interest in religion declined, he helped shape a more secular ethical conception of socialism based on the dignity of human labour. This was not – as is often assumed in critiques of Morris – backward-looking or anti-technology, but established through the inherent creativity of this labour. It meant a continuous struggle, not just against capitalism – given its alienating effects on human creativity – but also left-wing utilitarianism and Fabianism in the battle to shape a just society.

'Give me love and work, these two only', said William Morris.[21] The purpose of life is to employ one's talent to useful, beautiful and meaningful ends. Work is about relationships. We inherit knowledge from the past and we shape it with others into new forms of value. Work creates hope. Morris described it as 'worthy work'. It carries with it the hope of pleasure in rest, the hope of pleasure in using what it makes, and the hope of pleasure in daily creative skill. All other work, he said, is mere toiling to live that we may live to toil.

For this ethical English Marxist tradition, socialist change was not simply political and economic change – the 'machinery' of socialism, as Morris famously called it – but heightened consciousness to realize our true capacities: self-realization. In the cauldron of the industrialization of the late nineteenth century, with the creation of the ILP, it was a politics built to defend and promote an authentic human life and the struggle to advance a society that cultivates essential human virtues, a politics of fellowship. Socialism is considered as the fight against human degradation and the retention of human dignity, primarily in terms of human labour.

A Different Labour

The political conflicts of the late nineteenth century triggered a neo-classical revolution, whereby economic value was removed from labour into the scientific realms of utility and individual rational preferences. Socialist responses divided between Romantic and rational; ethical and economistic. On one side of the divide stood Morris and the secular ethical and religious concerns of the ILP, with Fabianism, utilitarianism and various scientific socialist and economistic strands on the other. This basic fault line became encased within the emerging Labour Party. Founded in Bradford in 1893, the ILP, brilliantly led by Hardie, had resisted left unity with the doctrinaire, scientific economism of the Social Democratic Federation (SDF) at the critical 1895 conference, because it sought to build a democratic, domestic, ethical, non-materialist socialist tradition.

The ILP generation of Hardie, Macdonald and Lansbury – the three religiously devout 'apostles' – established a labour identity descendant from both Morris, with his appreciation of human virtue, creativity and self-realization, and Christian socialist traditions; the ILP blended both. Yet by the 1930s, Auden's 'low dishonest decade', despite the long-standing ILP associations of both Lansbury and Attlee, internal victory was secured by the professionals, pragmatists and operators. The page turned away from the prophets towards the younger planners and economists such as Gaitskell, Jay and Durbin, the New Fabian Research Bureau and the XYZ Group under the general guidance of Dalton. It signalled a takeover by the middle-class Fabians with their policy-heavy utilitarianism and the defeat of the party intellectuals Cole and Tawney.

A recurring feature, therefore, in the history of socialism, Marxism and Labour, is this brittle relationship between economic and ethical traditions, shaped by contrasting approaches to human labour. Even when acknowledging the contribution of Tawney, Morris remains the most significant figure in English socialism in upholding opposition to economism, utilitarianism and scientific Marxism across the left. His influence reappeared through the New Left, especially in Thompson's biography and Williams's *Culture and Society*. He also provides a final link back to industrial relations pluralism.

Rethinking the Oxford School

In Guild Socialism, we can pinpoint a bridge between late nineteenth-century Romantic and religious concerns and later attempts to institutionalize a labour interest within the post-war British economy that we discussed in chapter 2. This tradition, influential in the early decades of the last century, echoed Morris's emphasis on human creativity in its arguments for greater industrial democracy through guild regulation of the labour process.[22] These ideas, looking back to the Middle Ages for inspiration, were expressed in the pages of the early Christian Socialist publication *The New Age*, which was pioneered in Arthur Penty's 1906 *Restoration of the Guild System*.[23] Penty, a follower of both Morris and Ruskin, later became an advocate of a 'distributism' that leant heavily on Catholic social teaching.

It is through the political and intellectual contribution of G.D.H. Cole, however, that the tradition was to find real influence. In 1915 Cole formed the National Guilds League and between 1917 and 1920 authored four books on Guild Socialism. His personal contribution, and the wider ideas regarding democratic workers' control, remained influential, inspiring a diverse group of writers and thinkers that included Tawney, Karl Polanyi and Michael Young, as well as New Left figures like Stuart Hall. Whilst its formal significance declined after the first few decades of the last century, the guild tradition remained a key reference point for more libertarian, democratic and anti-statist pluralist socialist and social democratic contributions throughout the last 100 years.[24]

Early adherence to guild socialist radicalism evolved into post-war corporatism, reflecting, according to Peter Ackers, a form of 'utopian pluralism' in its support for collective bargaining and economic stakeholding.[25] Key intellectual figures in this story of an exiled political tradition include Cole and Harold Laski, Walter Milne-Bailey within the TUC Research Department, Michael Young within Labour's Research Department, as well as Allan Flanders and Hugh Clegg. It is a journey from late nineteenth-century ethical socialism, especially in the work of Morris, to post-war pluralism in the representation of the labour interest.[26]

In this way the Oxford School, especially in the work of Clegg and Flanders, represents part of a generation's transition from pre-war radicalism towards post-war social democratic revisionism. It expressed a shift, often through direct personal wartime experiences, from left utopian to realist strands of thought in the face of both left and right-wing totalitarianism. Wartime had exposed these young radicals to the harsh realities of institutional democratic collapse and placed a renewed ethical emphasis on establishing pluralist balance within industry and new political, legal and social constraints over employment relations in the post-war era – just as it should do once more today, in order to confront the authoritarian populist threat by establishing a renewed emphasis on the dignity of labour.

Allan Flanders intellectually shaped post-war industrial pluralism,[27] but before the war was a full-time revolutionary follower of ethical socialist Leonard Nelson. In the 1930s he graduated towards a more mainstream Labour politics as the fascist threat intensified. Flanders was recruited to the TUC as researcher to support a team of economists including Cole, Evan Durbin and Joan Robinson, and subsequently Ernest Bevin to aid post-war reconstruction. In March 1949 he was offered a lectureship at Oxford. From then until his early death in 1973, Flanders stood at the intersection of two post-war traditions: as key theorist within an industrial relations community influential in government policy making and as contributor to the evolution of post-war social democracy and Labour revisionism.[28]

The work of the Oxford School can therefore be reclaimed within an anti-utilitarian socialist tradition. By the 1960s Flanders consistently linked early ethical socialist concerns within a practical programme to articulate the labour interest in the regulation of the economy. At Nuffield he evoked the language of Morris and 'fellowship' in criticizing a trade unionism built around a 'narrow materialism'. He distinguished his method form Crosland's utilitarianism and throughout the 1950s sought to counterpose ethical socialist values to material interests framed around the notion of the dignity of labour, equating the labour interest with that of the national interest.[29]

What emerges is a non-deterministic ethical left tradition vital in the physical creation and early leadership of the Labour Party. Its influence significantly diminished from the 1930s. Socialist humanist concerns that recognize the dignity provided by meaningful work, the need to civilize capitalism and regulate the employment relationship have informed a variety of non-utilitarian left traditions of justice. They could again today as part of a rebuilt telos. It is worth briefly reflecting on someone who could have been embedded within this tradition.

Footnote: Tony Blair – The Road Not Taken

Tony Blair lives in domestic exile. Within Labour an enduring hostility ensures the party is unable to own its recent history, the victories and achievements, and aids political opponents who want the same. On leaving office politicians tend to be defined by their last defenders, usually those present at the political death. Often these are the most blinkered adherents of what the leader had become – rather than what they had once been or promised to be. It is true of Thatcher and Blair. Blair's supporters narrowed what New Labour was and could have been. Yet Blair has hardly helped himself.

The man who held the hand of Clement Attlee when he died, Alfred Laker, noted that he 'had a depth of feeling he took care to keep hidden'. Attlee disguised his idealism, indeed Romanticism, in the creation of a distinct political persona. The same can be said of Tony Blair. The 'smiling public man' we see today, to borrow from Yeats, has sought to both obscure and redraw his political character to build a modern liberal, cosmopolitan identity. Tony Blair had once been inspired by different philosophical and spiritual concerns. Through an adherence to thinkers such as John Macmurray, he had sought to build a political appreciation of the common good. A distinct ethical approach was ever present before he became prime minister.

On 6 July 1983 in his maiden speech to the House of Commons, Blair argued that 'British democracy rests ultimately on the shared perception by all the people that they participate in the benefits of the common weal', a deliberate reference to William Morris. The common weal speaks to both individual fulfilment and mutual flourishing concerned with the dignity of the person and their dependence on others. Blair was no intellectual fool. In 1995, as leader, Blair echoed Tawney when suggesting 'socialists have to be both moralists and empiricists'. A year earlier, on accepting the leadership he said he was on a 'mission to lift the spirit of the nation . . . a country where we say, we are part of a community of people – we do owe a duty to more than ourselves . . . a country where there is no corner where we shield our eyes in shame . . . the power of all for the good of each . . . that is what socialism means to me.'

In the 1996 *Why I Am a Christian*, Blair disowned utilitarianism and demanded a return to ethics to reclaim this element of party history. Earlier, in a 1995 speech, these concerns anchored a story of national renewal and the patriotism of his 'Young Country'. That same year he was embracing the 'moral reformers' of Tawney and Morris, Cobbett and Owen. In a private handwritten note sent to Cardinal Basil Hume in October 1996, following the publication of the Church's document on 'The Common Good', Blair talks of 'the essential dignity of every person', of solidarity and personal responsibility, and contrasts this with modern, individual, liberal economic rationality. Throughout Blair consciously aligned Labour's approach to justice with deeper spiritual concerns. In 1994 he argued for a new national mission: 'A new spirit in the nation based on working together, unity, solidarity, partnership. This is the patriotism of the future. Where your child in distress is my child, your parent ill and in pain is my parent, your friend unemployed or homeless is my friend; your neighbour my neighbour. That is the true patriotism of a nation.' This terrain lies beyond economic liberalism or a remote cosmopolitanism – the territory of Blair's later reinvention. His early preoccupation was ethics. His speeches read like modern parables refracted into stories of national renewal and shared sacrifice. They echo the concerns of Kennedy, Johnson and Bush.

Such thinking informed the radicalism of Labour's first term, in confronting poverty pay, literacy and numeracy challenges and nurturing the notion of citizenship and the Sure Start agenda, before the latter was truncated by Brown into a strict utilitarian welfare-to-work scheme. Internationally it was reflected in the pursuit of human rights and the establishment of a dedicated department for international development now buried into the Foreign Office by Boris Johnson. This ethical architecture helps account for the extraordinary emotional power, grip and reach of New Labour in that period. A radical hope was forged before it turned to real anger as Blair and New

Labour rewound back to utility and calculus, the party's historical comfort zone. People had invested in something that promised to be different and they were humiliated and felt played when it wasn't delivered.

Tony Blair has consciously buried his early political character. His autobiography is a deliberately elusive book.[30] He barely mentions his ethical concerns – apart from a few pages in chapter 3. Here, and with great subtlety, Blair splits and reunites spiritual and political thinking through a consideration of his ideas. First, he counterposes religion, which 'starts with values that are born of a view of humankind', and politics, 'which starts with an examination of society and the means of changing it'. He then argues he has always seen the latter through the prism of the former: 'I begin with an analysis of human beings as my compass; the politics is secondary.' Such insight never appears again in the 768 pages of text. His autobiography, his own story, dis-invents himself and his early ethical concerns as if to hide what he lost. It is a sad backfill. It is almost as if it is too painful for him to return to the source of his emotional power and success. It amounts to self-harm in the way he diminishes who he once was.

Blair's ethical socialism challenged left economism and rebuilt a sense of the common good. It wasn't to last. Blair redrew himself in defence of an international liberal order. At home New Labour's early concerns were crowded out by the applied utilitarianism of the Treasury. Domestic politics tended toward the transactional, the allocative, the rational management of unending growth. The language became colder, more functional – until the music stopped and the money ran out.

Unwittingly, the most telling description of what Blair lost had been contained within New Labour's own bible: Philip Gould's *The Unfinished Revolution*.[31] Here Gould makes a revealing distinction when he describes his parents as having 'wanted to do what was right, not what was aspirational'. The possibility that these were not mutually exclusive was never entertained. It signals how the pollsters reoriented Blair's earlier ethical approach to human activity and aspiration. In the pollsters' view, aspiration consisted of the impulse to accumulate and consume without regard to the consequences for others or any sense of responsibility to society. Over time, this view defeated Blair's early humanist fusion of spiritual and political thinking. In short, the economists and the pollsters defeated the ethics of the early Blair.

In its place was constructed a politics that considered people as atomized and individualistic; as unsentimental and ruthlessly self-interested. It assumed that the electorate – or at least the section of it that counted – held fast to a rationality that verged on the misanthropic. By 2001, New Labour's policies were essentially based on a mythical 'Middle England', drawn up by the pollsters and located somewhere in the South East, built around continuous growth and affluence and where politics always had to be individualized. In the end New Labour assumed the electorate would only respond to a sour, illiberal politics about consuming more, rather than deeper ideas of fraternity, of collective experience, and what it is we aspire to be as a nation. The territory that Blair had defined was gradually vacated. New Labour lost its soul.

Contrast the Blair of 1994, with his emphasis on nation building and of forging a left patriotism, with where he ended at the 2005 party conference. Here he coldly described how 'the character of this changing world is indifferent to tradition. Unforgiving of frailty. No respecter of past reputations. It has no custom and practice.' Rather than view this world as destructive and dehumanizing, he celebrated those who are 'swift to adapt' and 'open, willing and able to change.' Within a few years Blair's language had descended into a brutal liberalism. Blair's genius was in excavating a politics deep within Labour history. Yet tragically, the character of Blair – and of the governments he led – shifted from such ethical concerns towards rational economic and political utility and calculus. By 2005 what worked for Blair was a 'liberal

economy, prepared constantly to change to remain competitive'. What developed was a dystopian 'winner takes all'
vision of capitalist modernity in which the human values
of commitment, fidelity and loyalty were subordinated
to anonymous and unpredictable market forces with its
'creative destruction' of ethical values, social cohesion and
cultural identity. By the end, New Labour's utilitarianism
cultivated an acquisitive, selfish individualism cut loose
from social obligations. The early virtues disappeared, as
did the duties and obligations; the sense of community.
Labour lost its moral purpose and language, its hope and
optimism as it detached from the lives of the people.

9

Human Labour and Radical Hope

A Culture Dies

Ron Todd died of leukaemia in April 2005. His funeral was held at Dagenham and Redbridge FC complete with a British Legion, Naval Association and Marine Guard of Honour. The youngest son of market traders, Todd left school at 14. Following national service, he briefly became a gas fitter before joining the Dagenham Ford plant where he stayed until 1962 when he was appointed a full-time officer for the TGWU. Later he became Regional Secretary, National Organizer for the automotive sector and finally General Secretary, until retirement in 1992. The last speech he made was just a few weeks before his death, in front of forty people in Dagenham Labour Hall, on the threat of the far right at a pre-election event sponsored jointly by the local party and anti-fascist group Searchlight.

When Todd started at Dagenham, more than 40,000 people worked directly in the plants, with tens of thousands more employed across vast supply chains. Vehicle assembly ceased in 2002, leaving just the engine plant. By the time he died, employment at Ford had dropped to just

3,600. Over 100,000 local jobs linked to manufacturing were lost throughout the post-war era.

Historically, the families of numerous Ford workers lived on the Becontree Estate, some 27,000 properties in the middle of the borough, the largest public housing project in the UK, possibly Europe. In 1981 almost 90 per cent of the borough housing was council-owned. Over the next 20 years half the council stock, mostly houses rather than flats, was bought by tenants at vastly reduced rates. Some used the properties as investments, many sold up and moved out, triggering extraordinary inward migration. By 2005 the estate was on the front line in a country-wide battle against the far right. Heightened insecurity and anxiety amongst local people flowed from rapid deindustrialization, diminished housing prospects through 'right to buy', enduring poverty and extraordinary demographic change. What for many were once secure local landmarks of work, housing, family and kinship were now threatened.[1]

New Labour disappointed Ron Todd. In his final speech he rocked with emotion railing against the lack of decent jobs, trades and rewarding work. Alongside limited housing and an eroding sense of community, the stage was set for extremists to ratchet up, scavenge and racialize the growing sense of grievance. The foundations of a working-class economy and culture were disintegrating with little being done to manufacture jobs, housing or political hope, in turn creating a rich seam for the fascist right.

The British National Party, formed after a split inside the National Front in 1982, remained a marginal force in British politics until an influx of asylum seekers and predictable tabloid backlash in the 1990s. Its first electoral breakthrough came in a council by-election for the Millwall ward on the Isle of Dogs in September 1993, following a successful 'Rights for Whites' campaign. Despite an increased vote, they failed to hold the seat in full council elections the following May.

In 1994 the BNP founder John Tyndall polled 7 per cent in a Dagenham by-election, following the resignation from

Parliament of Bryan Gould. In 2004, two years after the end of car production, in the Goresbrook council ward – directly across the A13 from the plant – the BNP secured a 52 per cent share of the vote, with Labour on 29 per cent. In their first victory since Millwall, they successfully combined anger over lack of social housing with hostility to new immigrants. The BNP claimed the council was operating a secret 'Africans for Essex' policy, giving £50,000 grants to African families to move into the borough. At the General Election a few days after Ron Todd's death, they took 16.9 per cent of the vote in Barking, their best election result.

The following Easter, the Barking MP Margaret Hodge gave an interview in which she claimed, 'When I knock on doors, I say to people "are you tempted to vote BNP?" and many, many, many – eight out of ten of the white families – say "yes"'. Naturally every newspaper sent journalists along the District line to ask the people of the borough why they harboured such feelings and the BNP rose in the polls.

On local election day 2006, the BNP stood thirteen candidates in the fifty-one seats. With long queues in warm sunshine, twelve of their candidates won; with more standing they would have taken the council. They averaged 41 per cent in their seven wards compared to 33 per cent for Labour. They became the official opposition on Barking and Dagenham Council with control of the whole authority and Westminster seats in their sights. It was no freak result. In the 2008 London Assembly elections, they topped the polls in eight of seventeen wards with leads of up to 18 per cent. The next year at the European elections they gained 19.4 per cent and UKIP 14.8 per cent. Things looked desperate.

Radical Hope

What can be done when a culture dies? The psychologist Jonathan Lear's study of 'radical hope' suggests the key is the avoidance of despair and whether a community can create new meaning by drawing on its cultural traditions.[2] Referring to the experiences of the Crow Indians, Lear enquires how a community can avoid destruction in circumstances where the practices that give life meaning no longer remain.

Shortly before he died, the Crow leader Plenty Coup explained 'when the buffalo went away the hearts of my people fell to the ground, and they could not be lifted again. After this nothing happened.' The culture died. According to Lear what was lost was 'a liveable conception of the good life' – the destruction of the telos.

We have seen the consequences of such cultural death amongst indigenous communities in patterns of addiction, abuse and violence. Lear's approach has provided a different way of thinking about those communities that disintegrated following the decline in coal and steel production in North America.[3] It also connects with an emerging 'deaths of despair' literature – declining life expectancy amongst middle-aged white Americans without college degrees linked to opioid use, suicide and addiction. For analysts Case and Deaton, the underlying reasons for these deaths stretch beyond questions of material wellbeing. They reflect how lives have become increasingly meaningless, linked to the decline in the traditional demand for labour amongst the US white working class.[4]

Yet politicians have difficulty understanding this collapse. Modern capitalism imposes these breakdowns on once-stable communities wrapped in a language of 'progress' and modernity and the necessary embrace of 'globalization'. Today the agile, meritocratic winners are those who can reinvent themselves – the educated, networked and resourceful. By 2005 Blair made a virtue of those swift to adapt – to change jobs, retrain and re-educate. Technological determinists also have little appreciation or empathy for such trauma; their motor driving history justifies the collapse of once-stable patterns of work by conceiving of such change as inevitable and beyond political contest, or even something that should be 'accelerated'.

The culture that provided meaning and purpose for the Crow died. Their belief system was destroyed; the loss was irreparable. What could come next? Lear suggests genuine renewal must resist despair and respond in ways that draw strength from tradition. *This is not nostalgia but a condition of resilience and survival.* The Crow survived because the leadership reimagined a future – even though they didn't know what that was. This is what Lear means by the notion of *radical* hope, of a future without guarantees. Borrowing from Plato, it is hopeful in wishing for something not necessarily understood. This form of leadership demands courage – the key political virtue.

Reimagining the dignity of work can help the avoidance of despair in communities that have experienced a cultural death, like Dagenham. More generally this can also help a political movement reimagine its own future by drawing on tradition and memory in the search for a new telos and in so doing sustain communities once understood as its 'base'. For the Crow, work – hunting and war – were practices that consumed the whole population – as the chief said, 'after this nothing happened'. Lear remains confident that human beings have the capacity to come back from such experiences; he has a faith in humanity in its resourceful resilience. Condemned to such cultural loss, humans can reimagine a life.

Can modern communities suffering a human toll through cultural breakdown reimagine a future? Is this kind of radical hope possible when political leaders have such difficulty appreciating the feelings of their fellow citizens? Most of the time the political class implies it is doing the victims a favour – widening horizons and opportunities, re-equipping them, offering more training and welfare. Can politics today create radical hope?

The Political Interregnum

How do you disentangle legitimate grievance from ugly intolerance and unacceptable behaviour? This moral dilemma shaped the Dagenham political terrain for years. A decade later, before pandemic, it became an international challenge as authoritarian populism marched across the planet destabilizing the foundations of liberal democracy. A virus and deep recession now threaten to further upend our political systems. The unequal employment effects of the pandemic and threats of renewed austerity ramp up the prospects of populist revolt. Have we the political resources to navigate this interregnum? We can draw some conclusions related to questions of work and economics, ethics and justice.

Utility

Dagenham is a good political test bed. It is regularly used to showcase a story of political hopelessness, one that laments a disappearing working class through deindustrialization; an argument that accounts for both Brexit and Trump. Take, for instance, the way Dagenham has been used alongside Youngstown, Ohio, to open a new academic portal into populist anger through the decline of car and steel production, culminating in the 2016 European referendum and US elections.[5] This concentration on shifting work profiles is useful, yet reveals limitations with utilitarian justice.

Such analysis tends to focus on material inequality remedied through welfare, education and training reforms to help 'post-industrial' communities and the 'left behind'. These concerns for distributive justice dominate the political narratives of both the radical and social democratic left. They seek to both understand and resolve the motivations behind populist discontent through addressing the material conditions experienced by people and communities. Such approaches are welcome but insufficient and underwhelming given the challenge.

Economic factors are obviously significant; the 2008 crash and austerity demonstrated as much. Dagenham disquiet predated the crash, revealing how a thirty-year neo-liberal experiment overpromised and failed to deliver. Any enduring political solution must re-engineer an inclusive growth. Yet an over-reliance on distributional issues can appear indifferent to the wider emotional wellbeing of citizens and the lives they wish to live. This is not just restricted to questions of neo-classical utility but also afflicts progressive utilitarian traditions.

This leads to a second problem, why one form of distributive reform should be ranked above another. If a certain outcome, a level of material equality, is desired to achieve a measure of fairness, why rank a tax credit over a job, or a UBI over another social security reform? If, like Adam Smith, you consider work to be an instrumental necessity in order to enjoy the rewards – such as freedom, consumption, joy – why is this best achieved with a job rather than other welfare options that provide similar opportunities? People value work over welfare, the data is overwhelming. Yet in remaining agnostic on the means to secure a certain distribution of outcomes, policy makers miss this and fail to understand the feelings generated when left unfulfilled. At a minimum, work is a decorative source of dignity and its loss humiliating. Yet as we have seen, this basic insight and reality tend to be neglected in politics.

Economic liberalism failed to deliver in Dagenham. But distributive justice might not offer enough. The community cannot be genuinely known through such a restricted lens. The community was created by work and its history only understood through the dignity and communion work has provided and sustained and the appalling consequences when it has been lost. It has never been indifferent or agnostic on the subject. This was a problem for the Treasury under New Labour, which sought to remedy deindustrialization and real wage decline with welfare reform and tax credits. On one level a dramatic arc from *Made in Dagenham* to *Fish Tank* speaks to what work offers in shaping personal wellbeing and relational strength, collective vitality and resilience and the dystopian fallout when lost – a descent from humiliation into nihilism. Utilitarian social democracy remains too technocratic, instrumental and blinkered to comprehend such visceral responses.

Technology

The other New Labour response to income inequality was supply-side reform driven by determinist assumptions of technological change and the future demand for labour. This process culminated with Blair's 2005 conference speech where he celebrated those 'swift to adapt' and 'open, willing and able to change'. Within New Labour, the diagnosis supplied by Leadbeater reoriented the government away from traditional post-war concerns to confront capital and regulate labour. Today, the more radical left has also succumbed to a similar liberating vision of our technological future. With New Labour antecedents, we are gripped by chronocentric overconfidence replacing a moral imperative to regulate work.

In some variants a new educated network elite will dominate employment, in others no one will have to work. For the latter, we appear beholden to a post-work futurology to demand full automation and UBI, the logical endgame of Brown's tax credits. We either equip citizens for new knowledge employment or enter a world of workless abundance. Here populist disquiet – although turbulent – is considered transitional if we educate, equip or compensate people sufficiently to navigate a bright future.

Over the last twenty years, through a specific approach to technological change and work futures, dominant parts of the left have sought to reset progressive politics and regularly bid farewell to the working class. Meanwhile following a pandemic, the 'left behind' working class are everywhere – they never actually went away – and their value to us and the affection shown to them immeasurable. We clapped for them instead of waving goodbye.

The problems don't end here. Much of the left assumes technological change guarantees a new left progressive coalition amongst the urban educated networked youth. Happy amongst our new 'base' with our language of education, liberty and opportunity we risk valorizing university education and retaining a meritocratic tendency to inadvertently impose harsh judgements on those who fall outside such definitions of success; those less 'swift to adapt' and the work that they perform, which historically afforded personal status and standing.[6] People identify this in the character of modern progressive politics – it is hardly hidden – and politically react when they realize it disrespects them and their families, their beliefs and traditions, their jobs and communities.

More generally the dignity of traditional work has, until a pandemic struck, been whittled away in an economic era that attached status to making money and acts of public consumption. Now after the experience of virus and death the value of such work has been recognized and once again been invested with moral purpose. Yet technological determinism has left the progressive left woefully out of position to benefit from these shifts. In this changing world it is the left that needs to be 'open, willing and able to change' in again recognizing the dignity of labour.

Cosmos

Work historically defined the left. It was the political representative of the working class and the communities built to house their labour power. Yet the possibility of a politics anchored around ideas of work and community is dissolving across the social democratic and socialist left of today.

In February 1998 the sociologist of the 'third way' Ulrich Beck offered us the 'Cosmopolitan Manifesto'.[7] He suggested the basis for a new 'world citizenship' and 'ethical globalization' with two key stages in this entrenched modernity: the first, the legacy of freedom captured through various civil rights struggles; the second, brought on by our modern dissolved attachments where 'community, group and identity structure have lost their ontological cement'. Old progressive values have been replaced by a radical individualism, especially amongst the well-educated and the young, expressed through emerging global 'cosmopolitan parties'. These parties reflect three broad political movements within and between nation states: first, a modern appeal to transcendent human values that appear in every culture and religion – 'liberty, diversity, toleration!'; second, an emphasis on global political action over local or national interventions; and third, attempts to democratize transnational regimes and regulators. A mixture of technological and normative factors is helping forge a new left global politics amongst the post-national, urban, networked, educated youth. This new political constituency has replaced the workers.

Once again Blair's liberals join forces with today's radicals. A recurring theme of both the pragmatic and radical left over the last twenty years has been the role and appeal of dramatic technological change in establishing a renewed utopian left imagination. This links the New Labour approach to the New Economy and globalization with today's radical 'tech-utopian' approach to the 'new' New Economy of machines and platform capitalism. In *Empire*, Hardt and Negri highlighted the limited significance of the sovereign nation given the amorphous power of capital whose modern rule suggested the declining relevance of territory and country. What was emerging was *empire without the significance of nation*. For today's left this has brought forward the political possibilities offered by a transnational *multitude* to condition and challenge global capital – a radical new form of political agency. This is where modern Marxist technological determinism takes us – a new global left in place of a discernible working class.

This form of cosmopolitanism asserts a privileged global citizenship over other attachments, such as patterns of work, community or nation. Yet politicians seek a mandate from a specific piece of territory and have particular moral obligations to an electorate, at least their constituents think they do! There is, of course, a totally coherent position that holds that all global citizens have equal economic and social rights – we have suggested in these pages a transcendent human dignity – yet the danger is to surrender to the populist the currency of politics; of place, community and nation. This can bend towards disrespect of those fearful of the forces of globalization – and those communities destroyed by them – and derision towards a desire for home, work and community, characterized as nostalgic, or worse still reactionary.

Yet just as the working class has reappeared, so too has the nation state, not least in resetting national labour markets. A renewed corporatism produced a bordered furlough politics brokered with the TUC. National states have re-emerged as employer and purchaser of last resort. Across Europe a pandemic has reasserted borders to ensure containment. State aid rules were parked and national state spending in breach of European controls allowed. The idea of an alliance between the nation and the working class is not yet dead.

Rights

A final point relates to statecraft. Liberal reason, non-judgemental state neutrality and the withdrawal from moral judgement in arbitrating the political square give the appearance that progressives disengage from the fundamentals that feed the populist right: questions of worth, esteem, resentment and humiliation. We inhabit a world detached from the everyday concerns of the people we purport to represent, using a language of rights, opportunity and fairness too underpowered in its ability to capture people's feelings. A few years ago Michael Sandel suggested:

Liberal neutrality flattens questions of meaning, identity, and purpose into questions of fairness. It therefore misses the anger and resentment that animate the populist revolt; it lacks the moral and rhetorical and sympathetic resources to understand the cultural estrangement, even humiliation, that many working class and middle class voters feel; and it ignores the meritocratic hubris of elites.[8]

To sum up, until very recently the value of work was neglected. It appeared that everything other than work generates value: capital, technology, risk taking, innovation, anything other than accomplished work and skilful cooperation with others. The crash of 2008 revealed the consequences of an economy too often rewarding vice in the form of cheating and greed rather than vocation and virtue. The pandemic has forced us to re-engage with the dignity of labour. Yet the modern left is ill-equipped to do this given the ascendancy of utilitarian and rights-based traditions, aligned with an endemic technological determinism, leaving it with limited resources to re-establish a politics of work. Even though the clue should be in the name, today it is Labour's opponents that appear better placed to secure such a new politics.

The Right

Is modern conservatism the descendant of the neo-classical politics of Thatcher and a revolutionary thirst to deregulate labour or will it become the new workers' party, eager to fill the space vacated by Labour, the party of the new global multitude? The jury is out.

Today the inheritors of the radical intentions of *Stepping Stones* can be found in the pages of *Britannia Unchained*, a short, 2012 edited collection from a group of young, then unknown, right-wing Tory MPs including Kwarteng, Patel, Raab, Skidmore and Truss. It received some unfavourable attention – newspapers picked up on the suggestion that the

British people are 'among the worst idlers in the world', too many of whom 'prefer a lie-in to hard work'. The authors demonstrate socially liberal credentials on race, sexuality, gender and identity, yet retain a destructive economics to take on the compassionate conservatism then occasionally visible around Cameron. The state is always malign and the labour market never flexible enough. Reform means marketization and intensified commodification. In this world, safety nets stifle a 'can-do' culture, weakening our work ethic and muscular individuality. Banking crises are simply part of the natural order of things; Britons are working fewer hours because they can't be bothered or are wilfully avoiding work. The contributors were all part of the right-leaning Free Enterprise Group. Theirs is a binary world, where everything is forward or back, progress or decline, sink or swim, good or bad. The choice is between regulation and dynamism: their ideal worker is one prepared to work long hours, commute long distances and expect no employment protection and low pay. Their solution to the problem of childcare is unregulated, 'informal and cheap childminders'. They demand dramatic cuts in public expenditure matched by equivalent tax cuts. The demonization of the welfare recipient is everywhere. Community, society or indeed country is always trumped by textbook liberal economic concerns. The European Union performs the function that the unions had 35 years earlier.[9] This looked to be the future of conservativism until Brexit changed everything.

With Cameron gone, the new prime minister set up the Taylor Review of working practices in an attempt to reset conservatism by bolstering her political bona fides amongst the leave-voting working classes. The opening lines of the 100-page report detailed its ambition: 'The work of this review is based on a single overriding ambition: All work in the UK economy should be fair and decent with realistic scope for development and fulfilment'. Amongst other recommendations, it proposed a new status of employee, the development of 'good work', a crackdown on 'exploitative' conditions and weak management to confront Britain's productivity challenges. The launch revealed May's desire for a conservative rethink:

> The nature of employment is central both to our national economic success, but also to the lives we all lead ... A good job can be a genuine vocation, providing intellectual and personal fulfilment, as well as economic security ... With good work can come dignity and a sense of self-worth. It can provide good mental and physical health, and emotional well-being.

And later: 'If we are to deliver our vision for Britain as a high-wage, high-skill economy then we know that we have to invest in good work'. She then listed past labour market interventions – the National Living Wage, minor enforcement measures, adjustments to zero-hours contracts, extended flexible working and shared parental leave and the usual celebration of labour market statistical success – numbers in work and unemployment rates – to reinforce the contrast with Thatcherism and the 1980s Tory legacy. Then came nothing in terms of actual policy follow-through. An interest in industrial democracy, for putting workers on the boards, was floated but came to nothing and soon she was gone.

The 2019 election saw Labour's 'Red Wall' breached and successful appeals to 'Workington Man'. Boris Johnson's victory came from winning over the lowest-paid and least-educated, older voters and Labour leave voters. Before the pandemic he appeared intent on becoming the party of work and the activist state. Regional Keynesian stimulus through infrastructure spending on houses, bridges and railways. A New Deal sentiment was detectable. A substantial economic role for the state was already established by their election victory and the importance of work, workers and the working class will not pass with the virus but will remain a central part of a new evolving conservatism. With a pandemic, it reappeared in new dialogues with the unions and an 80 per cent wage furlough.

However, government mishandling of the pandemic might well now undermine the ambitions of a core Tory team intent on rewiring conservatism around a new politics of work; right-wing orthodoxy and austerity could once again emerge as the default position. These remain dangerous times for the left, it cannot just rely on Johnson screwing it up. It must urgently rediscover a politics of work. However, the fashionable left response is to head entirely in the opposite direction and replace a politics of work with the case for maximum welfare through UBI.

Universal Basic Income

Why?

UBI is a big, powerful idea. Advocates swear by it. Before the pandemic, amongst a growing vocal movement, it emerged as the economic and social antidote to automation; after the virus struck many embraced the idea to remedy the fallout from contagion.

All sorts of people, often bitter political opponents, think it's an idea whose time has come. This elasticity means it's an elusive idea.[10] UBI is generally understood to mean a regular, state-administered, universal unconditional payment.

Historically, the arguments for a basic income were theological rather than ideological – fulfilling the Christian duty of charity – derived from belief in a shared human inheritance. Practical interventions tended to fall short of the modern definition of UBI, however. Systems of historic relief for the poor and care for the vulnerable were often funded by *personal contributions* rather than through taxation administered by a central state apparatus. In many early formulations, the minimum income was generally not considered universal, available only to those in need, and often *conditional* on their willingness to work.

A series of left-wing arguments have been made in favour. It clearly appeals to a left utilitarian or distributional argument for maximizing the welfare of the maximum number of citizens. Some argue it reinforces the disutility of capitalist employment and helps resist the commodification of labour. It nurtures 'unalienated', non-market labour as traditional, exploited work becomes relatively more expensive and helps the bargaining power of workers by altering their disposable income. At first sight it is difficult to reconcile UBI with Marxism; with its focus on distributional issues that bypass traditional concerns with ownership of the means of production, distribution and exchange. Yet as a Ricardian Marxism has prioritized distributional contests over workplace politics, so UBI has become more attractive for sections of the radical left.

Yet UBI is also rejected on the left. In common with utilitarian left-wing thinking in general, many believe it underplays the democratic qualities that should characterize a just society, truncating politics towards questions of maximizing welfare. It oversimplifies and standardizes economic and social need through a universal monetary figure, triggers 'freerider' concerns, and underplays the significance that contribution should play in building a just society. Citizenship consists of deeper relations, duties and obligations to fellow citizens – questions of fraternity – above and beyond the passive receipt of an individual money transfer.

Liberal arguments in favour of UBI include the libertarian desire for individual freedom and release from an over-mighty state bureaucracy and collectivized public services. From a more progressive perspective, it can express a basic human right to a certain level of subsistence and help remedy economic and social disadvantage. In classical Rawlsian approaches, the *difference principle* – respecting inequalities if they don't negatively affect the disadvantaged – can include UBI as a foundation of justice. There is also a liberal argument, traced back to Thomas Paine, that UBI respects the shared human inheritance of all citizens, although this doesn't necessarily make a specific case for UBI over other forms of asset or capital transfer.

UBI can also appeal to those operating within republican or virtue-based traditions of justice. It is seen to secure freedom from domination, not least in employment, or provide the freedom in time and resources to help citizens to flourish, live a good life and participate and contribute to a just society. Yet because of inherent 'freerider' concerns, neglect of a contributory principle and sense of reciprocity, it might also be considered unjust. From an alternative feminist standpoint, the case for UBI has been made in terms of challenging the idea of the male breadwinner and the character of domestic labour.

The idea has political support on the radical right. Milton Friedman advocated a not dissimilar negative income tax to overhaul public services and roll back the state. Charles Murray saw UBI as a vehicle to aid the consumer and intensify the commodification of society, not just labour, by dismantling public services, labour and social security protections. UBI offers the prospect of real freedom by replacing the architecture of the welfare state with a personalized fiscal transfer.

To left-wing advocates it offers precisely the opposite. It complements rather than substitutes for welfare systems and labour market protections; an integral part of radical economic, social and democratic packages. For some advocates, UBI separates wage labour from income, and thereby confronts the very nature of capitalism and capitalist reproduction. For others, it simply acts to correct in-work poverty or the bargaining power of labour.

Other advocates of UBI claim political neutrality and suggest it offsets the unequal consequences of automation, enduring labour market segmentation and flatlining wages while retaining the consumer drivers needed to bolster modern capitalism. UBI will distribute what the robots, AI and machine working will produce.

The point is that UBI is difficult to assess in terms of competing theories of justice or on a simple divide between left and right. One might think, however, that its confident utopian advocates on the left should remain cautious when their most committed opponents are also likely to support the idea in order to secure radically different outcomes.

Technical Concerns

There are mundane, practical issues that confront advocates of UBI. Is it financially feasible? Is it more effective in securing what its advocates desire compared to say Sovereign Wealth Funds, Federal Job Guarantee Programmes or Universal Credit? How has it operated in practice? Who benefits and who does not? What would be its effects on other aspects of public policy and the operation of welfare systems and labour markets? What policies need to accompany UBI to ensure the policy achieves what its advocates consider as desired outcomes?

There is a growing body of evidence of the costs and effects of UBI through a variety of economic models and studies of pilot programmes. Yet much of this analysis is inconclusive. For example, whilst the IMF, the OECD and the UN Special Rapporteur on poverty have all recently highlighted the economic difficulties in achieving a decent UBI, this has been challenged by, amongst others, Compass, research for the then Shadow Chancellor John McDonnell, and the RSA. This literature basically concludes that affordability is linked to the level of the UBI; it costs more to introduce a generous payment and this in turn shapes the concrete effect. The scale of ambition appears to define both its cost and consequences.

There is a basic category issue regarding citizenship and the defined community with UBI. The notion of community is being challenged in modern politics for its exclusiveness, often by cosmopolitan traditions and global rights approaches to citizenship, freedom and justice – regularly amongst the most passionate advocates of UBI. Yet the policy is administered by a central state apparatus and requires a defined, bordered political community in which citizens can enter and leave. Advocates of UBI therefore must grapple with the politics of migration, free movement

and modern 'insider/outsider' dilemmas that bedevil progressive politics but are fundamental to any successful
redrawn social contract.

There are some compelling arguments in favour, especially in the work of Philippe Van Parijs, although there
are major hurdles to overcome. Arguably the most per-
suasive pragmatic, practical case for UBI has recently been
made by Louise Haagh. She has suggested that to survive,
UBI needs to be rescued from the hands of the polemicist,
populist and reductionist, not least because UBI has caught
the imagination at a time both of rising inequality and
nationalism alongside deep austerity. This has created a
solve-all or solve-nothing debate around the idea, whereas
the strongest case for UBI is part of an overall anti-poverty
strategy rather than as a utopian magic-bullet antidote to
modern capitalism.[11]

The Real Case against UBI – The Dignity of Work

The case against UBI is best made by inspecting the
assumptions of those advocating the policy. Today most
fashionable support for the idea follows from deterministic assumptions of technological change and the end of
work, or at least the inevitable degradation of modern
work, especially amongst analysts who tend to instrumentalize employment. Yet technology is not destiny – if
it were, we might all support UBI. If work were to end,
the case for UBI would be much stronger than if full
employment was feasible. If politics matters, and could
help create good, purposeful, rewarding work, then the
case for UBI would be less overwhelming than in a world
of inevitable 'bullshit' jobs. If people retain instrumental
views about work, the case for UBI in achieving levels
of distributional justice is higher than if we believe work
to be fundamental to humanity and a vital source of
declarative dignity.

Today the basic case for UBI is to offset future structural
unemployment given technological change and automation.

Yet despite the noise generated, there is no evidence that work will end; the picture is more mixed, messy and political. Literally there is no compelling evidence that the robots are taking over at the expense of work as we know it. Whilst the case for automation-induced mass unemployment has regularly been made down the ages, it has never turned out the way people have predicted. It is a political contest. In the UK before the virus struck, we had the highest levels of employment for over forty years. After the pandemic, worked stopped, and we had the biggest welfare intervention in history to furlough workers – a UBI test drive. Nothing is predestined. UBI was advocated before the pandemic as a response to automation and after to remedy a virus. You can accept and support UBI as a short-term remedy to correct a unique short-term shrinkage in work, but also believe such a collapse should be used to once again challenge capital and rebuild the nature of work.

If the end of work is coming because of technology rather than biology, when will this be expressed in the productivity and employment statistics? If labour is finished, should we not be seeing at least some evidence of this through a substantial technological boost to our productive performance? This story of epochal change rests uncomfortably with the realities of our escalating productivity malaise or 'puzzle'.

What is crucial is what is revealed behind the back of the UBI debate – profound disagreements about what is of value to us and the contribution of others in terms of the dignity of human labour. Even if technological change is wiping out millions of jobs, should we just accept this? If we believe in the dignity derived from good work, should we not show respect for our fellow citizens and organize industrially and politically for decent job and income guarantees, collective rights, strong unions and decent public services, rather than a vision of mass welfare with UBI?

There is therefore a strong case against UBI if you believe the statistics and methods prophesying an end of work to be fundamentally flawed, if you believe the nature of work and its future character to be inherently political questions and reject a politics over-reliant on questions of distribution and utility, and if you recognize the intrinsic value of work in the lives of people – corroborated by all the survey evidence available. This approach suggests UBI retains destructive properties – it robs people of meaning and dignity in their lives, leaving them more isolated, vulnerable, angry and humiliated, and society less fraternal and solidaristic; it provides an atomized neo-liberal endgame of isolated consumption with citizens transformed into the ultimate passengers of capitalism. Arguments referring to materially just outcomes secured by UBI or its support for liberal individual freedom and self-realization are operating with very different criteria of political success and visions of what is just. An idea which for some overflows with utopian socialist possibilities can for others represent a dystopian nightmare.

Much fashionable interest in UBI on the left makes a compelling case for rejecting the idea because of the indignities of a life without purposeful work. Can we imagine an alternative?

The New Work Covenant

Within a few months of the onset of Covid-19 our labour was politicized in ways thought unimaginable during the decades when work was decoupled from politics. In a matter of days, a tiny virus upended economic history. A job was no longer a rational individual trade-off between work and leisure, a simple market transaction, because the market stopped. The role of the state was redefined. Out of necessity, a Tory government had to step in to regulate who works, where and under what conditions.

Not only that but corporatism reappeared. The TUC emerged at the centre of economic life for the first time in over forty years to help shape the most significant labour market intervention of living memory – a state furlough programme. The status and significance of human labour were visibly re-established and situated at the centre of political, economic and social life. Everything changed. We realized the market is not the only thing that can provide and define work; we have greater political choice over the future of work. Before the pandemic struck, governments of both left and right had sunk into a bewildered stasis, unable to reimagine a politics of work.

Today the 'labour question' is once again centre stage. Questions of utility have defined politics over recent decades, so can a pandemic crisis help shape a new politics concerned with human dignity, especially human labour? Could the dignity of labour provide a new telos for the left and the organizing principle for a new approach in government after Covid-19?

Although this book is about work perspectives rather than policy, it is worth asking what type of labour regulations might follow such a reorientation and fit alongside an economic programme of infrastructural development, devolution, and civic and regional renewal. Throughout we have been critical of utilitarian and Ricardian tendencies to focus on distributional questions rather than a politics of work and the labour process. Historically, on the left under the guise of 'labourism', these approaches tended to stake a claim for workers to receive more for the fruits of their labour. Yet as we discussed, during the last Labour government this was effectively jettisoned in favour of more supplementary welfare. Today this has culminated in the case for UBI and automated luxury which decouples reward from work altogether. An alternative approach would seek to enhance human dignity and re-establish the ethical case to reward vocation and the contribution of labour as well as nurture good-quality work and challenge and democratize the organization of the labour process itself – by turning to the neglected question of industrial democracy.[12]

The Promotion of Good Work

The United Nations Economic and Social Council defines 'decent work' as that which 'respects the fundamental rights of the human person as well as the rights of workers in terms of conditions of work safety and remuneration ... respect for the physical and mental integrity of the worker in the exercise of his/her employment.' The case for Good Work has been made, amongst others, by the Taylor Review, the Report of the Future of Work Commission convened by then Labour Deputy Leader Tom Watson and the ongoing work of the Harvard GoodWork Project.

The Skills and Employment Survey identified worker autonomy, influence and discretion over work, responsive management, initiative taking, innovation and high-impact suggestion making as key productivity drivers, yet all have been in retreat since 2006. These remain useful Good Work benchmarks.

A new government-sponsored *What Works Centre* should be established to research, define and promote Good Work, including across the multiple arms of the state and its supply chains. The 2006 Companies Act should be reformed to place obligations on companies to provide Good Work. Specifically, section 172 of the Act should include clarity within defined articles of association for the provision of Good Work and employment standards. A new Labour government should immediately embrace and promote as an act of public policy a new Good Work Covenant, the contents of which might include the following:

Good Work Covenant
1 *Right* – Everyone should have the right to good work.
2 *Fair reward* – Everyone should be paid fairly.
3 *Decent conditions* – Everyone should work on decent terms and conditions.
4 *Equality* – Everyone should be treated equally and without discrimination.

5 *Dignity* – Work should promote human dignity.
6 *Autonomy* – Work should promote autonomy.
7 *Wellbeing* – Work should promote physical and mental wellbeing.
8 *Support* – Everyone should have access to institutions and people who can represent their interests.
9 *Participation* – Everyone should be able to take part in determining and improving working conditions.
10 *Learning* – Everyone should have access to lifelong learning and career guidance.[13]

The Renewal of Vocation

To restore dignity and pride into the world of work means recognizing and rewarding vocation – calling. The pandemic has taught us that it is the vocational workforce that must shape a new community and nation and underpin any emerging industrial strategy. For a brief period during the pandemic, we acknowledged this work and cannot now forget.

Many remain in insecure and low-paid professions. For instance, nearly a million work in care, mostly women, often from ethnic minorities. Many are agency workers, regularly on zero-hours contracts, very poorly paid – half receive less than a real living wage. The care of the elderly and vulnerable is now recognized as a vital vocation. As a career, it should be the source of stable, secure work.

We will need a system of education, skills and professional development to cover, amongst others, retail, transport, energy and the utilities, public services, the construction trades, planning and surveying, green jobs in housing, recycling, land maintenance and associated skills, education, health and wellbeing, sport and recreation, childcare, residential and domiciliary care, digital skills and design. Career progression, reward and work quality will need to be overhauled across these sectors.

The 2016 Sainsbury Report revealed a jungle of some 20,000 courses delivered through 160 providers. The twenty-five T-Levels, rolled out over the next few years, could be the long-term solution in creating a highly skilled vocational workforce, yet they remain pegged to the A-level gold standard and could fail just as NVQs, TVEIs and others have.

The future should learn from the failures of the past. Our obsessions with knowledge work meant that Tomlinson's 2004 Commission proved too hot to handle in recommending 14- to 19-year-unification with the integration of knowledge and skills qualifications. Future reforms should start from here with a unitary system of vocational and academic education.

Future change should ensure a formal collaboration to advance vocational provision between providers, unions, employers and government under a new National Council on Work Futures. Exam boards should be explicitly charged with the promotion of vocational qualifications. With scores of universities facing ruin because of the pandemic, we should take this historic opportunity to properly reintegrate the higher and further education sectors. For instance, the 1992 polytechnics and degree-awarding colleges could be tasked with the integration of the theory and practice of academic and technical education.

To further advance the vocational sector, we should consider the incorporation of law colleges and teaching hospitals, along with further education and university technical colleges. We should ensure greater professional autonomy and status for the guilds and new national colleges of skilled work and professions. We should establish more national and royal colleges so as to acknowledge the calling and contribution of our vocational professions. The renewal of the vocations should be a core organizing principle for the next Labour government.

A Voice for Labour

The dignity of labour refers not just to rights in law but security and personal sanctity, autonomy and voice at work. In Germany, workers can establish a works council and in larger companies help elect the supervisory board. So, too, in Denmark where workers have rights to cooperate and appoint worker directors. Yet industrial democracy has never been a priority for the dominant utilitarian traditions within Labour and the unions.

The only concerted consideration of industrial democracy in the UK came with the Bullock Committee, established by Harold Wilson in response to the European Commission's draft Fifth Company Law Directive to harmonize employee involvement across the continent. The final Bullock Report in 1977 was split. All companies with over 2,000 employees were to have worker representatives. Union members could vote for supervisory board candidates, although the minority report proposed a second-tier board. In 1978, a tepid White Paper was introduced including statutory consultation rights for workers in companies with over 500 employees and it went nowhere.

Industrial pilots have been attempted, famously by shop stewards at Lucas Aerospace. Worker cooperatives were initiated at Meriden Motorcycles, Kirby Engineering and Scottish Daily Express, and worker directors experimented with in British Steel and later the Post Office.

Mrs Thatcher opposed EU initiatives in preference for privatization with occasional employee share option sweeteners, later unsuccessfully dusted down by George Osborne in the 2013 Enterprise Act.

Economic democracy has fared little better. In 1992, Labour rejected attempts to include 'Worker Ownership Funds' in its manifesto to redirect profits into worker corporate stakes. Under Corbyn, Labour reheated these ideas, proposing 10 per cent of shares in companies with over 250 employees be allocated to employees, with dividends going to the state.

Tony Blair provided another missed opportunity. The 1998 Company Law Review and 2001 White Paper eventually led to the 2006 Companies Act which stated directors should 'have regard to' other stakeholders, yet retained the underlying supremacy of shareholder interests. Reporting requirements on companies to make clear how they served non-shareholder interests had been dropped in 2005.

Democracy at work could be the 'Big Idea' for Labour with codetermination at the centre of economic strategy. A change in the understanding of company purpose should inform any revival of social democracy whereby companies adopt a corporate purpose beyond the pursuit of shareholder value.[14] Directors should be empowered to pursue the success of the enterprise in which long-term shareholders and workers have a common interest. This would include a transfer of sovereignty over takeover decisions from shareholders to directors and workers. For instance, the consent of workers should be required for takeovers recommended by directors. Parent companies should be held liable for the obligations of their subsidiaries and supply chains.

At a minimum, democratic reform of industry would adapt section 172 of the 2006 Act to ensure statutory duties in the interests of all stakeholders in long-term company stewardship. Further reform could begin with new works councils like French *comité d'entreprise* in companies with over fifty employees and industrial democracy experimentation and worker-director pilot schemes across the public sector. Pilot Worker Golden Shares and worker-directors should be a condition in any post-pandemic corporate bail-outs.

Personal Dignity and Integrity

The pandemic has brought unprecedented mass biological checks and tracing, reminding us again of the need for personal safeguards given modern surveillance capitalism and the effects of digital Taylorism.

Upholding personal dignity in employment would include, at a minimum, the right to mental privacy in employment, including against unknown intrusion to know our thoughts, constraints on the use of personal data by employers without meaningful consent and the ability to associate without surveillance.

Further reform would include the right to own personal data, the right to fairness and non-discrimination in algorithmic decision making and rights to information and consultation ahead of technological restructuring.

The New Worker

The Taylor Review achieved little. Established by Theresa May in 2016 to consider mechanisms to reconcile flexibility and fairness in the labour market, it proposed a new category of worker that was at once too limited and complex.[15] About 10 per cent of the labour force work for digital platforms and up to 10 million work in some form of precarious work. But, as recently noted, it gave 'no serious consideration to the changing conditions of employment in low-wage, labour-intensive industries such as garment manufacture', nor did it 'probe the position of workers in the large warehouses that pump prime the businesses of Amazon, Sports Direct or Asos' and it was largely 'devoid of any systematic empirical evidence' and offered 'few if any recommendations that might be judged a threat to the direction of travel of many high-profile, internet or platform-based companies'.[16]

Post-pandemic recession is throwing up more insecure, zero-hour workers who switch their labour across employers. In future much of this will be carried out within homes, stretching the modern work panopticon beyond a traditional job and location.

All should operate under a new statutory single definition of worker decoupled from contractual status. This would align the rights of all employees and other categories of worker with day one protections including sick and holiday pay and, post-pandemic, full PPE and the ability not to work in unsafe environments – a right to stop the job.

We should institute a New Covenant for Key Workers. This would recognize their contribution and guarantee a basic package of rewards including pay and protections, together with a range of new entitlements including housing, travel and access to public services to establish a new social contract for essential workers.

The New Deal

Article 23.1 of the Universal Declaration of Human Rights states that: 'everyone has the right to work, to free choice of employment, to just and favorable conditions of work and to protection against unemployment'.

The right to work has been recognized in several international legal instruments – including ILO Convention 159 – as fundamental to the promotion of human dignity, material wellbeing and fostering personal development and recognition within the community. The right to work has been elaborated by Articles 6, 7 and 8 of the International Covenant of Economic, Social and Cultural Rights, which deal respectively with the right to gain a living, the right to fair and favourable conditions and the right to form trade unions for all human beings.

In terms of the practical application of such sentiment, the Works Progress Administration created during the Great Depression put 8.5 million Americans to work, erecting more than 600,000 miles of new roads, building 100,000 bridges and viaducts, and constructing 35,000 buildings. During his State of the Union address on 11 January 1944, Franklin D. Roosevelt called for a second 'economic bill of rights', to guarantee political rights – to housing, medical care, education and social security – into the constitution beginning with the 'the right to a useful and remunerative job'. The plan went largely unfulfilled. However, today in the US the most dramatic new idea is arguably not that of UBI but a radical job guarantee programme being promoted by politicians such as Cory Booker, Kirsten Gillibrand and Bernie Sanders, think tanks like the Center on Budget and Policy Priorities and Centre for American Progress, and academics including

William Darity Jr at Duke and Darrick Hamilton at the New School.

With the prospect of enduring recession and having seen what is politically possible with the Job Retention and Income Support schemes for the furloughing of work and to help the self-employed, the time has come to establish a new *Work Covenant*. To start the process, a new Pandemic Reconstruction Force for Jobs and Growth in every region could oversee a new one-year jobs guarantee with accredited training, living wage or the union negotiated rate. This would be funded by national government, but delivered at regional and local level by councils, unions, business and Jobcentre Plus. Special emphasis would be placed on community action programmes, especially ecological regeneration.

This should be only the beginning, however. Within the first term of a new Labour government, a new *Right to Work* should be enshrined in legislation – the right to a useful and remunerative job for every citizen. Every citizen should have the right to decent work in safe conditions that is properly rewarded. This might include a new Climate Army as part of the proposed Green New Deal. Given the cost and the practical difficulties of creating such a large number of jobs, the progressive think tanks should all join forces to begin to work through the details of such an unprecedented job guarantee programme in anticipation of a new Labour government.

Many argue that full employment is a political impossibility, that a reserve army to discipline labour and retain control over the labour process is inevitable, usually based on a deterministic reading of the origins of neo-liberalism. Consequently, many prefer distributional solutions such as an indefinite furlough scheme – as a proto UBI rather than work guarantee programme. Any job guarantee programme would be linked to other rights and protections to stop benefit-plus and workfare schemes. Every citizen should be guaranteed decent work. After the pandemic, this is now a question of political will.

Work at the Centre of Government

Under a new Labour government, a new Department for Work should embed the dignity of labour throughout government. This would include establishing new employment standards and supply chain compliance in public contracts across national and local government. Such a department would overhaul the inspectorate and penalty regime within the new integrated Labour Market Enforcement body covering labour law, gig economy regulation, modern slavery, gangmasters and minimum wages.

Statutory union recognition procedures should be reviewed and trigger membership thresholds reduced. As a priority, Schedule 11 of the 1975 Employment Protection Act should be revised to transfer 'recognized' terms and conditions of employment into unrecognized areas.

The department should also develop a new evidence base to guide policy making. This would involve at a minimum the refunding of the Workplace Employment Relations Study (WERS), which had served governments well between 1980 and 2011 before it lost support under Cameron and Osborne.

A New National Work Assessment

Other countries can do it: we have had, amongst others, the German Industry 4.0, the Danish Disruption Council, the New Zealand Future of Work Forum, the Swedish Job Security Council. We require a tripartite National Council on Work Futures as part of an ongoing dialogue; a new National Work Assessment. Such a body would be required to address ethical questions posed by new technologies and the obligation to uphold the integrity of the person. In the immediate period the council would be tasked with developing a new tripartite agreement on post-furlough bail-outs with anti-redundancy clauses and labour regulation standards for all those receiving government support.

The new council in association with ACAS would seek

to encourage sectoral social partnership dialogue covering employment, skills, training and productivity. It would revise the ACAS redundancy code to ensure consultations with works councils before dismissal. It would also be required to re-establish the WERS and an enhanced national research capacity on modern work. As we have mentioned, no original research was carried out for the Taylor Review of modern working practices.

In conclusion, the basic overall point is simple. The next Labour government should be organized around the moral imperative to reorder our economy and society in recognition of the dignity of labour. This could establish the foundations of a desperately needed new public philosophy for the left – a new telos – and inform a renewed conception of the good life. It can be done, but requires the necessary political will.

Epilogue

There is a fashionable tendency across the left to write off the working class. They are situated on the wrong side of history and will inevitably be wiped out by automation. They are demonized as an angry, violent, intolerant, racist crowd, easily manipulated by the authoritarian populist right – vividly displayed throughout Brexit. In his first post-election analysis,[1] the author of *PostCapitalism*, Paul Mason, suggested that after four defeats 'something fundamental has changed in the dynamic of British politics, requiring the left project to be redefined and a new alliance of progressive forces to be formed'. Labour lost because 'the nativist narrative was coherent, clear and emotionally grounded. Against it, Labour had nothing effective'. Here an inherent nativism has been welded onto the backs of the 'left behind'. This is where technical, often impenetrable debates within economic theory, especially Marxism, take us politically today. A selective reading of value theory provides a precise reading of modern history and the future direction of politics. It is a politics that threatens to detonate the left and undermine Labour.

For adherents of this approach, the 2017 and 2019 elections represent a 'Brexit realignment', with a strong

Labour vote share among younger voters and graduates, in urban metropolitan areas and amongst social classes ABC1. Recent shifts in voting patterns validate abstract theories of a new left; the emergence of a progressive cosmopolitan multitude. As such, quietly and without any debate, technological determinism is destroying an identifiable left politics. Fashionable orthodoxy stretching from New Labour to Corbynism through a certain reading of history affirms Labour should ditch a sentimental attachment to a working class encased in 'traditional' heartlands. The meaning of the word 'traditional' has been altered. It now signposts a white demographic and nativist sentiment and no longer retains a classical left usage to define a long-term, or 'traditional', relationship to the means of production and the reproduction of labour power. For Mason, attachment to this 'traditional' base is considered ethically intolerable and anyhow offers diminishing electoral returns. This slice of the electorate is physically older, literally dying out and, due to epic technological change, will no doubt never be replaced.

We are told there exists a radical Labour-supporting cultural demographic residing within a new political geography. Labour should hold its nerve and accept casualties in its 'traditional' seats as we transition towards our new heartlands, safe in the knowledge that the working class is withering away and doesn't vote for us anyway. The new 'base' of the left is to be formed around 'networked individuals' residing in 'Remainia'; the left has youth, technology, the sites of future growth and an entrenched liberal modernity on its side. The progressive future is bright; the global, urban networked youth have replaced the workers.

Have they though? This is a big bet. It rests on both a theoretical and demographic determinism, where, within its defeats, Labour is thought to be actually winning, by retaining a linear understanding of history inherited from a misreading of Marx and the LTV. Technology is not destiny. It also rests on the selective use of data in support of the end of work and the working class; the data simply doesn't back up the march of the machines. The future of work remains a contested political terrain. Yet such fashionable thinking and talk of 'post-workerism' is destroying the foundations of left-wing politics in a post-pandemic world where the moral significance of work and human labour has renewed meaning and greater physical visibility. It should not need to be said but political parties do not just exist to chase votes. They are traditions built around competing theories of justice and democracy; yet today, flimsy argument, determinism and technological conjecture threaten the essential character and purpose of the party, even its existence. To charges of nativism and inevitable realignment, we should respond with a renewed faith in humanity. For even after Brexit and deindustrialization, evidence from places like Dagenham offers radical hope when built around the dignity of labour.

In early 2010, with a worsening economy, escalating public debt following bank bail-outs and austerity, Labour was plummeting in the polls. Yet during those same months, across Barking and Dagenham, the BNP was outfought and out-organized in what – according to Hope Not Hate – was the most intense and successful anti-fascist campaign in British history. The BNP was annihilated. Standing thirty-four candidates, enough to take control of the council, it lost every single seat – and lost them badly. Labour won all fifty-one seats on offer, with some of its candidates receiving double or even treble the votes of their BNP rivals.

It proved to be the decisive moment for the BNP. Splits emerged, divisions widened and bills were left unpaid. Within a few months Nick Griffin was challenged for the leadership and although he clung on, his party was shattering all around him. By 2014 he had lost his European seat and been deposed. Their defeat in Barking and Dagenham was the beginning of the end for the most successful far-right party in Britain.

Forward wind a decade. Having retained all fifty-one council seats in both 2014 and 2018, in 2019 Labour held on in Dagenham and Rainham as the 'Red Wall' fell, despite being the top Tory London target with a 70 per cent leave vote and a key marginal seat since 2010 boundary changes. The popular caricature of Dagenham and Rainham is one synonymous with deindustrialization, the collapse of Dagenham 'Fordism', racism, the BNP, UKIP and Brexit. Seen in these terms, it should have been 'Exhibit A', the prime casualty, in the long march towards the bright new left heartlands. Based on indicators such as age, patterns of work and education and race, the community corresponds to the stylized image regularly deployed in identifying 'left-behind' communities and 'traditional' Labour seats.

Yet Dagenham was one of the very few leave-supporting areas where Labour defeated the Brexit Party in the 2019 European elections. Over recent years it has consistently bucked the national trends. This followed dramatic organizational renewal when the 'Red Wall' was first challenged over a decade earlier by the BNP. Locally, Labour was more resilient when Johnson targeted the community post-Brexit. A simple lesson is that rather than writing off these 'traditional' communities, Labour should learn from its recent history and focus on organizational reconnection with them.

There is a bigger problem for Labour beyond organizational renewal. The party's ideological range has collapsed in recent years. This is not just a simplistic approach to technology and recourse to the lazy fiction of immanent utopias. It is a preoccupation with distributional issues which limits any real appreciation of what is driving today's anger, resentment and populist energy. This is especially the case in terms of the dignity of labour and its role in shaping community that remains beyond the reach of a remote liberal cosmopolitanism and a rights-based neutrality when assessing the boundaries of justice.

In stark contrast, political renewal today in Dagenham is being constructed on the community's historic foundations of work and the desire for human dignity. Through council-led regeneration, primarily in reclaiming older automotive, chemical and energy sites, massive housing and infrastructural rebuild is underway, creating tens of thousands of decent local jobs. The community is literally being rebuilt through reimagining an economic future different from its past but equally ambitious. One built on work. Housing and infrastructure are aided by a series of relocating universities, major high-tech film and digital investments, new green technologies and cultural interventions, alongside investments across the Ford estate in the technologies required after the demise of the combustion engine. It is a story of economic transition and massive investment nurtured by an innovative local state which retains local memory. It is an ongoing renewal of labour. Over the next few years, a major part of London guild history – Billingsgate, Smithfield and New Spitalfields markets – will all be relocating into the borough, bringing many thousands more new jobs and with it vocations and training centres, dramatically resetting the local demand for labour and patterns of skill formation. It is a long way from *Fish Tank*.

Jonathan Lear believes, in our very nature as finite human beings, we long for things that we do not yet fully understand. This form of desire takes courage and is rewarded with hope – hope that is 'radical' because it transcends our ability to understand what this new kind of life will be. It approximates a spiritual hope but is not necessarily religious and invests great belief, resilience and strength in people and their communities. Humans can resist a meaningless life born of an economic and cultural death. It is worth concluding with a final return to *Fish Tank*.

The film captures a humanity that is beyond utilitarian politics. The film can be read as an honest, redemptive story about the dignity of human labour. Workless dispossession, nihilism and interpersonal brutality are everywhere on a dead-zone estate which was once inhabited by the strongest working-class labour movement in post-war British history. Today the drama depicts how wretched, empty lives are disrupted by an outsider; a strong confident desirable worker. This breach reveals in Mia a latent capacity for love and the fraternity she has never experienced in a world decaying around her. She survives and transcends her environment and forgives. Andre Arnold's essential humanism builds a radical hope not through a sense of technological imminence or a politics reset around young urban educated cosmopolitan winners but through an everyday tale of family, fraternity and work amongst a working class in outer East London. In the face of economic and cultural devastation, it provides a truly redemptive story about the capacity for love and fulfilment, of a new politics of the common good that rests on the dignity of human labour.

Notes

Prologue

1 Compare the emphasis of Mark Fisher's 'Capitalist Realism' with the utopian narratives of Paul Mason and Aaron Bastani. M. Fisher, *Capitalist Realism: Is There an Alternative?*, Zero Books, 2009. P. Mason, *PostCapitalism: A Guide to Our Future*, Penguin, 2015. A. Bastani, *Fully Automated Luxury Communism: A Manifesto*, Verso, 2019.

2 The 'Mardyke' has since been demolished and rebuilt as 'Orchard Village' and became a national example of dodgy new-build housing regeneration; see J. Harris, 'Leaking sewage and rotten floorboards: life on a "flagship" housing estate', *The Guardian*, 6 February 2017. https://www.theguardian.com/society/2017/feb/06/life-flagship-housing-estate-orchard-village-east-london.

3 The respected Electoral Calculus website overestimated Labour's national support yet calculated a Tory majority of 5,923 votes in Dagenham and Rainham.

Chapter 1: Work and the Modern World

1 Politics as translated from the Greek to mean 'affairs of the city'.

2 D. Harvey, *The Condition of Postmodernity: An Enquiry into the Origins of Cultural Change*, Blackwell Publishing, 1991, p. 240.

3 D. Goodhart, *The Road to Somewhere: The New Tribes Shaping British Politics*, Hurst, 2017.

4 In this introductory chapter, we use the terms 'work' and 'labour' interchangeably. In later chapters we separate 'labour', 'work' and 'employment'.

5 I tend towards the parochial. Seamus Heaney referring to his fellow poet Patrick Kavanagh thought of parochialism as permission to 'dwell without cultural anxiety among the usual landmarks of your life'. S. Heaney, 'The placeless heaven', *The Massachusetts Review*, Vol. 28, No. 3, 1987, pp. 371–80.

6 J. Bloodworth, *Hired: Six Months Undercover in Low-Wage Britain*, Atlantic Books, 2018.

7 This is not to ignore work being published in journals such as *New Technology, Work & Employment* and *Futures of Work*. These contributions are important. The argument simply acknowledges the general success of liberal economics in neutralizing what used to be described as the 'labour question'.

8 No original research was carried out for the 2017 Taylor Review of modern working practices compared to the extensive programme that informed the Donovan Royal Commission in 1968 or the high-quality survey and case study research programmes overseen by the then Department of Employment until the early 2000s. The National Board for Prices and Incomes (1965–70), the Commission on Industrial Relations (1969–74), the Bullock Committee on Industrial Democracy (1975–7) and later the Low Pay Commission from 1997 all initiated substantial pieces of independent research into the world of work. See W. Brown, 'The Donovan report as evidence-based policy', *Industrial Relations Journal*, Vol. 50, No. 5–6, 2019, pp. 419–30.

9 P. Mishra, *Age of Anger: A History of the Present*, Allen Lane, 2017, p. 330.

10 R.S. Foa, A. Klassen, M. Slade, A. Rand and R. Collins, *The Global Satisfaction with Democracy Report 2020*, Centre for the Future of Democracy, 2020. The Hansard Society, *Audit of Political Engagement 16*, 2019.

11 M. Sandel, 'Populism, Trump and the future of democracy', *Open Democracy*, 9 May 2018.

12 Andrew McAfee and Erik Brynjolfsson, *The Second Machine Age: Work, Progress and Prosperity in a Time of Brilliant Technologies*, W.W. Norton and Company, 2014.

13 M. Ford, *Rise of the Robots: Technology and the Threat of Mass Unemployment*, Oneworld Publications, 2016.

14 Carl Frey and Mike Osborne, 'The Future of Employment: How Susceptible Are Jobs to Computerisation?', Oxford Martin School Working Papers, September 2013, University of Oxford.

15 Daniel Susskind and Richard Susskind, *The Future of Professions: How Technology Will Transform the Work of Human Experts*, Oxford University Press, 2015.

16 'How robots change the world: what automation really means for jobs and productivity', *Oxford Economics*, June 2019.

17 Ian McEwan, *Machines Like Me*, Jonathan Cape, 2019. Similar themes have recently been played out in films such as *Blade Runner 2049* and *Ex Machina*.

18 A. Huxley, *Brave New World*, Chatto & Windus, 1932. G. Orwell, *Nineteen Eighty-Four*, Secker & Warburg, 1949.

19 Also see E. Davies (ed.), *Economic Science Fictions*, Goldsmiths Press, 2018. Contributors discuss the relationship between science fiction and economic narratives, with many arguing the positive case for using science fiction to reimagine how technology overturns neo-liberalism.

20 See especially R. Mackay and A. Avanessian (eds), *Accelerate: The Accelerationist Reader*, Urbanomic, 2015. N. Srnicek and M. Williams, *Inventing the Future: Postcapitalism and a World Without Work*, Verso, 2016.

21 D. Graeber, *Bullshit Jobs: A Theory*, Allen Lane, 2018.

22 H. Reed and S. Lansley, *Universal Basic Income: An Idea Whose Time Has Come?*, Compass Publications, 2016.

G. Standing, *Basic Income: And How We Can Make It Happen*, Pelican Books, 2017.

23 M. Taylor, *Good Work: The Taylor Review of Modern Working Practices*, UK Crown Press, 2017.

24 In February 2018, the ONS suggested that flatlining productivity since 2008 was due to more and more people working in unproductive industries such as food and drink services rather than more productive ones and to static labour mobility.

Chapter 2: The Labour Problem

1 References to the history of the Ford Motor Company and to post-war disputes throughout the rest of the book borrow from Huw Beynon's classic text *Working for Ford* as well as from local Dagenham testimonies from residents. See H. Beynon, *Working for Ford*, Allen Lane, 1973.

2 J. Dunlop, *Industrial Relations Systems*, Reinhart & Winston, 1958.

3 H. Clegg, 'Pluralism and industrial relations', *British Journal of Industrial Relations*, Vol. 13, No. 3, 1975, pp. 309–16. A. Flanders, *Management and Unions*, Faber and Faber, 1970.

4 We have not offered a detailed study of this tradition nor a thorough literature review. We simply seek to establish the key dividing lines in economics regarding the regulation of labour.

5 See especially chapter 5 in A. Smith, *An Inquiry into the Nature and Causes of the Wealth of Nations*, Strahan and Cadell, 1776.

6 D. Ricardo, *On the Principles of Political Economy and Taxation*, John Murray, 1817.

7 See, for example, K. Middlemas, *Politics in Industrial Society*, Andre Deutsch, 1979.

8 Inns of Court Conservative and Unionist Association, *A Giant's Strength: Some Thoughts on the Constitutional and Legal Position of Trade Unions in England*, Inns of Court Conservative and Unionist Association, 1958.

9 The first phase of the Oxford School contained five key figures: Hugh Clegg, 1949–66 Nuffield College Oxford,

1967–79 Warwick University, architect of final Donovan Report; Allan Flanders, TUC later Nuffield College and Warwick, key theoretician; Alan Fox, 1957–63 Nuffield Research Fellow; Bill McCarthy, PhD student under Clegg and Flanders, later Donovan Research Director and Nuffield Fellow, Labour employment spokesman in House of Lords 1980–97; Arthur Marsh, Senior Research Fellow Nuffield 1964–89. We should also acknowledge the contributions of Ben Roberts and John Hughes at Ruskin and legal theorist Otto Kahn-Freund. The second generation included George Bain, Willy Brown, Richard Hyman, Rod Martin and Roger Undy.

10　Recently this has been partly corrected with John Kelly's excellent interdisciplinary approach to the contribution of Allan Flanders (J. Kelly, *Ethical Socialism and the Trade Unions: Allan Flanders and British Industrial Relations Reform*, Routledge, 2011). We also await Peter Ackers' forthcoming biography of Hugh Clegg.

11　Report of British Royal Commission on Trade Unions and Employer Associations 1965–1968. HMSO, June 1968, Cmnd. 3623.

12　Pioneered in Allan Flanders' classic *The Fawley Productivity Agreements*, Faber and Faber, 1964.

13　Including showing a strikingly progressive attitude: 'Certain specific reasons which are not valid should be specified, namely trade union membership or activity, race, colour, sex, marital status, religious or political opinion, national extraction or social origin.' Coming several years before sex and race discrimination were specifically outlawed in employment. Religious discrimination was only outlawed in mainland Britain in 2006, and 'social origin' is still not dealt with by modern employment law.

14　When eventually implemented in the 1971 Industrial Relations Act, it contained a two-year qualifying period.

15　East London was again to the fore with the 'Pentonville Five' stewards jailed in July 1972 by Heath's Industrial Relations Court for their refusal to abandon picketing of the Chobham Farm container depot in Newham in support of the miners, leading to TUC calls for a general strike.

Chapter 3: Miracle Cures

1 An influence on current Downing Street incumbent Dominic Cummings, he later accused Thatcher of lacking political skills; their relationship suffered, and he left Downing Street in 1981. See A. Beckett, 'This is the man in No. 10 who inspired Cummings – and he didn't last long', *The Guardian*, 24 July 2020. https://www.theguardian.com/commentisfree/2020/jul/24/no-10-dominic-cummings-john-hoskyns-margaret-thatcher-whitehall?CMP=share_btn_link.

2 https://www.cps.org.uk/research/stepping-stones/.

3 At the time one of the most respected political interviewers on British TV whose Sunday lunchtime extended questioning of a politician often led the news.

4 Shadow Cabinet: Circulated Paper (Joseph, 'Notes towards the definition of policy'), 1975, Archive (Thatcher MSS), Declassified, House of Commons, MSS 2/6/1/156.

5 Space does not allow for a discussion of the contributions and differences between heterodox 'Austrian School' thinkers such as Hayek and their early influence on Thatcher and Joseph compared to orthodox neo-classicists like Patrick Minford who came later. The former promotes a politics of radical disruption, the latter one of marginal adjustment. Our focus here is on their shared methodological individualism and subjective theory of value and what this inspired in terms of a radical and enduring political reorientation when addressing questions of labour regulation in the UK since the 1970s.

6 J.K. Galbraith, *The New Industrial State*, Hamish Hamilton, 1967, p. 293.

7 Galbraith described them as 'defenders of the faith'.

8 Although this argument is disputed by economic orthodoxy, for a classic contribution on the origins of the factory and its organizational rather than technological imperatives, see S.A. Marglin, 'What do bosses do? The origins and functions of hierarchy in capitalist production', *Review of Radical Political Economics*, Vol. 6, 1974, pp. 60–112.

9 K. Korsch, *Karl Marx*, Russell & Russell, 1963, p. 45.

10 See K. Abbott, 'A review of employment relations theories and their application', *Problems and Perspectives in Management*, Vol. 4, No. 1, 2006, pp. 187–99.

11 J. Child, *British Management Thought: A Critical Analysis*, George Allen & Unwin, 1969.
12 See Beynon, *Working for Ford*, p. 341.
13 P. Nolan, 'The productivity miracle', in F. Green (ed.), *The Restructuring of the UK Economy*, Harvester, 1989.
14 See, for instance, G. Maynard, *The Economy under Mrs Thatcher*, Blackwell, 1988. D. Metcalf, 'Water notes dry up: The impact of the Donovan reform proposals and Thatcherism at work on labour productivity in British manufacturing industry', *British Journal of Industrial Relations*, Vol. 27, No. 1, 1989, pp. 1–31. J. Muellbauer, 'The assessment: Productivity and competitiveness in British manufacturing', *Oxford Review of Economic Policy*, Vol. 2, No. 3, 1986, pp. i–xxv.

Chapter 4: New Labour

1 For example, in the Viking and Laval cases. Case C-438/05, *Viking Line v. ITF* (11 December 2007); Case C-341/05, *Laval v. Svenska Byggnadsarbetareforbundet* (18 December 2007).
2 Competing approaches to justice and the history of the left are explored in part II.
3 J. Schumpeter, *Capitalism, Socialism and Democracy*, George Allen and Unwin, 1979.
4 C. Leadbeater, *Living on Thin Air: The New Economy*, Penguin, 2000, p. 126.
5 C.F. Sable, *Work and Politics*, Cambridge University Press, 1982; M. Piore and C.F. Sable, *The Second Industrial Divide: Possibilities of Prosperity*, Basic Books, 1984.
6 Full disclosure: I was one of those Downing Street officials.
7 D. Coats, *Raising Lazarus: The Future of Organised Labour*, Fabian Society, 2005. J. Cruddas, P. Nolan and G. Slater, 'The real economy not the new economy: The case for labour market regulation', in K.D. Ewing and J. Hendy (eds), *A Charter of Worker's Rights*, Institute of Employment Rights, 2002.
8 M. Campbell, S. Baldwin, S. Johnson, R. Chapman, A. Upton and F. Walton, 'Skills in England 2001 – research report', Department for Education and Skills, 2001.

9 D. Corry, A. Valero and J. Van Reenen, 'UK economic performance since 1997: Growth, productivity and jobs', Special Paper No 24. CEP/LSE, 2011.

10 A. Felstead, D. Gallie, F. Green and G. Henseke, *Productivity in Britain: The Workers' Perspective. First Findings from the Skills and Employment Survey, 2017*. Centre for Learning and Life Chances in Knowledge Economies and Societies, UCL Institute of Education, 2018.

Chapter 5: A Return to Marx

1 J. Fowles, 'On chronocentrism', *Futures*, Vol. 6, No. 1, 1974, 65–8.

2 This chapter draws on the following publications with Frederick Harry Pitts: J. Cruddas and F.H. Pitts, 'The politics of postcapitalism: Labour and our digital futures', *The Political Quarterly*, Vol. 91, No. 2, 2020, pp. 275–86; F.H. Pitts and J. Cruddas, 'The age of immanence: Postoperaismo, postcapitalism and the forces and relations of production', University of Bristol, School of Sociology, Politics & International Studies Working Paper Series, 2020 (01-20); J. Cruddas and F.H. Pitts, 'Marxism revisited', *Fabian Review*, Spring 2018, pp. 21–3. See also F.H. Pitts, 'The multitude and the machine: Productivism, populism, posthumanism', *The Political Quarterly*, Vol. 91, No. 2, 2020, pp. 364–72; F.H. Pitts, 'Beyond the Fragment: Postoperaismo, postcapitalism and Marx's "Notes on machines", 45 years on', *Economy and Society*, Vol. 46, No. 3–4, 2017, pp. 324–45; F.H. Pitts, *Critiquing Capitalism Today: New Ways to Read Marx*, Palgrave Macmillan, 2018.

3 R. Mackay and A. Avanessian (eds), *Accelerate: The Accelerationist Reader*, Urbanomic, 2014; N. Srnicek and A. Williams, *Inventing the Future: Postcapitalism and a World without Work*, Verso, 2015; P. Mason, *PostCapitalism: A Guide to Our Future*, Allen Lane, 2015; A. Bastani, *Fully Automated Luxury Communism*, Verso, 2019.

4 Key 'post-workerist' interventions include Negri's theorization of the social factory, Hardt and Negri's conceptualization of the new class subjectivity of the 'multitude',

Lazzarato's concept of 'immaterial labour', Vercellone and Virno's the 'general intellect', and Terranova's theorization of free labour. See M. Hardt and A. Negri, *Empire*, Harvard University Press, 2001; M. Lazzarato, 'Immaterial labor', in P. Virno and M. Hardt (eds), *Radical Thought in Italy*, University of Minnesota Press, 1996, pp. 133–50; T. Terranova, 'Free labor: Producing culture for the digital economy', *Social Text*, Vol. 18, No. 2, 2000, pp. 33–58; C. Vercellone, 'The crisis of the law of value and the becoming-rent of profit', in A. Fumagalli and S. Mezzadra, *Crisis in the Global Economy*, Semiotext(e), 2010, pp. 85–118; P. Virno, 'The ambivalence of disenchantment', in P. Virno and M. Hardt (eds), *Radical Thought in Italy*, University of Minnesota Press, 1996, pp. 13–36.

5 As we shall see, many who claim allegiance to Marx and the LTV advocate an approach to value, price and technology more in keeping with the assumptions of Ricardo than Marx. This has led some modern Marxist scholars to suggest the LTV should instead be reconsidered as a 'value theory of labour' to distinguish it from Ricardian traditions. This is the approach favoured in what follows, although to avoid confusion we continue to use the LTV description.

6 D. Elson (ed.), *Value: The Representation of Labour in Capitalism*, CSE Books, 1979, p. 145.

7 K. Marx, *Capital, Volume One*, 1976, ch. 7, pp. 288–307.

8 K. Marx, 'Preface', in *A Contribution to Political Economy*, Lawrence and Wishart, 1971 [1859].

9 See P. Anderson, *Considerations on Western Marxism*, Verso, 1976.

10 For the classic diagnosis of this tendency, see L. Colletti, *From Rousseau to Lenin*, New Left, 1972. The best defence of deterministic Marxism has of course been supplied by a philosopher rather than a value theorist, Gerry Cohen in his brilliant *Karl Marx's Theory of History: A Defence*, Clarendon, 1978.

11 The classic statement remains that of E. Bohm-Bowerk, 'Karl Marx and the close of his system', in P. Sweezy (ed.), *Karl Marx and the Close of His System*, Augustus, 1949.

12 In the light of Piero Sraffa's critique of Neo-Classical Economics and adaption of Ricardo's method in reducing all inputs to their embodied labour times through a dated labour

scheme, sympathizers such as Steedman attempted a general reconstruction of Marxist economics towards distributional conflicts over wages and profits as opposed to social relations within production. See I. Steedman, *Marx after Sraffa*, New Left, 1977. P. Sraffa, *The Production of Commodities by Means of Commodities*, Cambridge University Press, 1960.

13 H. Braverman, *Labour and Monopoly Capitalism: The Degradation of Work in the Twentieth Century*, Monthly Review Press, 1974.

14 Ibid., p. 86.

15 Ibid., p. 20.

16 Ibid., p. 169.

17 See, for example, M. Burawoy, *Manufacturing Consent: The Changing Labour Process under Monopoly Capitalism*, University of Chicago Press, 1979; A. Freidman, *Industry and Labour: Class Struggle at Work under Monopoly Capitalism*, Macmillan, 1977; R. Edwards, *Contested Terrain: The Transformation of the Workplace in the Twentieth Century*, Heinemann, 1979.

18 On today's left, the *Fragment* has taken the form 'akin to biblical exegesis', to quote Nick Thoburn, since gaining prominence in Negri's 1978 Paris lectures on the *Grundrisse*. See N. Thoburn, *Deleuze, Marx and Politics*, Routledge, 2003, p. 80.

19 A very good example of how abstract theoretical positions shape modern political debate is revealed by Aaron Bastani in a blog post on 13 June 2019 on the five 'must-read' texts to understand automation, the future of work and his popular take on 'automated communism'. Alongside three standard books on technological change – *The Second Machine Age: Work* by McAfee and Brynjolfsson, *Rise of the Robots* by Martin Ford and *The Economic Singularity* by Callum Chase – he bolted on the *Grundrisse* by Marx, specifically the *Fragment on Machines*. He argued, 'it is here where Marx not only isolates what technological change under capitalism means for working people, but how such transformation carries an immanent alternative for the "emancipation" of labour. While the older Marx would go on to repudiate his early work, including *The Grundrisse*, the last century has proven it a prescient account on the possibilities of technology.' Bastani repudiates Marx's own

repudiation of his earlier notebooks. His final choice was Keynes's 1930 'Letter on the economic possibilities for my grandchildren'. What is revealing is the elastic method which links orthodox modern texts on automation to assert a deterministic view of history based on a very precise, controversial Ricardian reading of Marxist value theory. See https://luxurycommunism.com/2019/06/13/five-must-read-texts-to-understand-the-future-of-work-and-automation/#. Upon such questionable foundations a whole strategy for the modern left is erected.

20 Mason, *PostCapitalism*.

21 P. Mason, 'The parallels between Jeremy Corbyn and Michael Foot are almost all false', *The Guardian*, 15 August 2016; https://www.theguardian.com/politics/commentisfree/2016/aug/15/the-parallels-between-jeremy-corbyn-and-michael-foot-are-almost-all-false.

22 Mason, *PostCapitalism*, p. 150.

23 Ibid., pp. 133–41.

24 P. Mason, 'Labour: the way ahead', Mosquito Ridge, 31 July 2016; https://medium.com/mosquito-ridge/labour-the-way-ahead-78d49d513a9f.

25 In his most recent work, however (P. Mason, *Clear Bright Future: A Radical Defence of the Human Being*, Allen Lane, 2019), Mason rejects both technological determinism and Althusser, in a journey back to humanism. This welcome rethink and focus on the role of human agency driving economic and social change rests uneasily with a continued Ricardian embrace of the *Fragment*. In chapter 8 we suggest a different route back to humanism.

Chapter 6: Dignity

1 It led the Marxist writer David Harvey to comment: 'I can't look at any discussion of technological change and imagine it's got some kind of socialist utopia attached to it, as you know some of these people writing these days do'. *Under the Skin with Russell Brand*, 15 January 2018.

2 'Would life be better if robots did all the work?' *The Public Philosopher* series, BBC, 7 March 2017. http://www.bbc.co.uk/programmes/b08gxndc.

3 J. Michaelson, K. Jeffrey, S. Abdallah and S. Mahony, 'Wellbeing at work: A review of the literature', New Economics Foundation, 2014; http://neweconomics. org/2014/03/wellbeing-at-work/.

4 Beynon's book was controversial, not least in depicting how a man lay dead on the Halewood factory floor for ten minutes while the line continued to run. Following publication, he received further communications from Ford workers about workers dying in the plant, including Tommy Turner from nearby Hornchurch who reportedly once lay dead on the Dagenham PTA line for 13 minutes.

5 H. Beynon, *Working for Ford*, Penguin, 1984, p. 391.

6 H. Braverman, *Labour and Monopoly Capitalism: The Degradation of Work in the Twentieth Century*, Monthly Review Press, 1974, pp. 51–2.

7 S. Heaney, 'Digging', in *Death of a Naturalist*, Faber and Faber, 1966.

8 See J. Rutherford, 'The future is Conservative', in *The Labour Tradition and the Politics of Paradox*, Lawrence and Wishart, 2011, pp. 88–106. D. Wordsworth and W. Wordsworth, *Home at Grasmere*, Penguin Classics, 1986.

9 J. Bate (ed.), *John Clare: Selected Poems*, Faber and Faber, 2004.

10 K. Polanyi, *The Great Transformation*, Beacon Press, 1957.

11 Again, see S.A. Marglin, 'What do bosses do? The origins and functions of hierarchy in capitalist production', *Review of Radical Political Economics*, Vol. 6, 1974, pp. 60–112.

12 V.I. Lenin, 'The immediate tasks of the Soviet government', in *Lenin Collected Works*, 2nd English edn, Progress, 1971.

13 For example, see M. Aglietta, *A Theory of Capitalist Regulation: The US Experience*, New Left, 1979.

14 The Five Dollar Day was introduced by Ford in 1914. It doubled the average wage, thus helping to ensure a stable workforce and also likely boosted sales as the workers were able to afford to buy the cars they were making. It laid the foundation for an economy driven by consumer demand.

15 R. Macklin, 'Dignity is a useless concept', *BMJ*, Vol. 327, 2003, pp. 1419–20.

16 S. Pinker, 'The stupidity of dignity', *The New Republic*, 28 May 2008.

17 This distinction is important and reappears throughout the history of the left. Whilst the secular humanist approach tends to consider dignity in ways not dissimilar to Macklin's belief in autonomy, religious interpretations offer a distinct conception of a human essence created by, and in the image of, God.

18 P. Hodgkiss, *Social Thought and Rival Claims to the Moral Idea of Dignity*, Antheum, 2018.

19 *Rerum Novarum*, Encyclical Letter of Pope Leo XIII on the Condition of Labor, Paulist Press, 1940.

20 *Laborem Exercens*, Encyclical on Human Work, United States Catholic Conference, 1981.

Chapter 7: What Do We Think and What's Going to Happen?

1 R. Sennett and R. Cobb, *The Hidden Injuries of Class*, Knopf, 1972.

2 R. Sennett, *The Corrosion of Character: The Personal Consequences of Work in the New Capitalism*, W.W. Norton, 1998.

3 For instance, in Z. Bauman, *Liquid Modernity*, Polity, 2000.

4 P.L. Berger and R.J. Neuhaus, *To Empower People: The Role of Mediating Structures in Public Policy*, American Enterprise Institute for Public Policy, 1977.

5 S. McKay and I. Simpson, *British Social Attitudes* 33: Work, 2015; https://www.bsa.natcen.ac.uk/latest-report/british-social-attitudes-33/work.aspx.

6 YouGov, 'How many Brits like their jobs and their wages', 3 August 2017; https://yougov.co.uk/topics/politics/articles-reports/2017/08/03/love-wage-balance-how-many-brits-their-job-and-the.

7 Commission Shift, 'Shift: The Commission on Work, Workers, and Technology – Report of Findings', New America Foundation, 2017; https://docsend.com/view/4wizcjb.

8 C.L. Ridgeway, 'Why status matters for inequality', *American Sociological Review*, Vol. 79, No. 1, 2014, pp. 1–16.

9 C. Tait, *A Good Day's Work*, Fabian Society, 2016; http://www.fabians.org.uk/wp-content/uploads/2016/11/Fabian-Society_A-good-days-work.pdf.

10 C. Thorley and W. Cook, *Flexibility for Who? Millennials and Mental Health in the Modern Labour Market*, IPPR, 2017; https://www.ippr.org/files/2017-07/flexibility-for-who-rep ort-july-2017.pdf.

11 New Economic Foundation, *Five Headline Indicators of National Success*, 26 October 2015.

12 TUC, *Insecure Work*, 29 July 2019.

13 University of Manchester 2011. http://www.manchester. ac.uk/discover/news/having-a-bad-job/.

14 S. McManus and J. Perry, *British Social Attitudes* 29: Work and Wellbeing, 2011. https://www.bsa.natcen.ac.uk/late st-report/british-social-attitudes-29/work-and-wellbeing/intr oduction.aspx.

15 Intergenerational Fairness Commission, *The Final Report of the Intergenerational Fairness Commission*, Resolution Foundation, 8 May 2018.

16 A. Felstead, D. Gallie, F. Green and G. Henseke, *Productivity in Britain: The Workers' Perspective. First Findings from the Skills and Employment Survey, 2017*, Centre for Learning and Life Chances in Knowledge Economies and Societies, UCL Institute of Education, 2018.

17 See chapter 7 in E. Anderson, *Value in Ethics and Economics*, Harvard University Press, 1993.

18 W. Hutton, *The State We're In*, Random House, 1995.

19 A. Felstead et al., *Productivity in Britain*.

20 J.M. Keynes, 'Economic possibilities for our grandchil- dren [1930]', in L. Pecchi and G. Piga, *Revisiting Keynes: Economic Possibilities for Our Grandchildren*, MIT Press, 2008.

21 A. Haldane, 'Labour's share', speech, Trades Union Congress, 12 November 2015; http://www.bankofengland. co.uk/publications/Pages/speeches/2015/864.aspx.

22 McKinsey Global Institute, *Harnessing Automation for a Future that Works*, January 2017; https://www.mckinsey. com/global-themes/digital-disruption/harnessing-automat ion-for-a-future-that-works.

23 R. Berriman and J. Hawksworth, 'Will robots steal our jobs? The potential impact of automation on the UK and other major economies', PWC, March 2017; https://www.pwc. co.uk/economic-services/ukeo/pwcukeo-section-4-automat ion-march-2017-v2.pdf.

24 I. Clark, 'Abandoned spaces and technology displacement by labour: The case of hand car washes', *New Technology, Work and Employment*, Vol. 33, No. 3, 2018, pp. 234–49.

25 M. Arntz, T. Gregory and U. Zierahn, 'The risk of automation for jobs in OECD countries: A comparative analysis', OECD Social, Employment, and Migration Working Papers 189, 2006, OECD.

26 D.H. Autor, 'Why are there still so many jobs? The history and future of workplace automation', *The Journal of Economic Perspectives*, Vol. 29, No. 3, 2015, pp. 3–30.

27 Trades Union Congress, *Shaping Our Digital Future*, TUC, 2017, p. 26.

28 HM Government, *Industrial Strategy: Building a Britain Fit for the Future*, White Paper, 2017, HM Government.

29 P. Brown, 'The prospects for skills and employment in an age of digital disruption: A cautionary note', SKOPE Research Paper No. 127, July 2018.

30 See P. Brown, H. Lauder and D. Ashton, *The Global Auction*, Oxford University Press, 2011; U. Beck, *The Brave New World of Work*, Polity, 2000; G. Standing, *The Precariat: The New Dangerous Class*, Bloomsbury, 2011.

31 A. Gorz, *Reclaiming Work: Beyond the Wage-Based Society*, Polity, 1999; J. Rifkin, *The Zero Marginal Cost Society: The Internet of Things, The Collaborative Commons, and the Eclipse of Capitalism*, Palgrave Macmillan, 2014.

32 S. Clarke, '"Atypical" day at the office: Tackling the problems of atypical work', Resolution Foundation, July 2017, http://www.resolutionfoundation.org/app/uploads/2017/07/Chapter_five_precarious_work-WEB.pdf.

33 G. Henseke, A. Felstead, D. Gallie and F. Green, *Skills Trends at Work in Britain: First Findings from the Skills and Employment Survey 2017*.

Chapter 8: Justice and the Left

1 https://www.jfklibrary.org/learn/about-jfk/the-kennedy-family/robert-f-kennedy/robert-f-kennedy-speeches/remarks-at-the-university-of-kansas-march-18-1968.

2 https://web.archive.org/web/20020602041420/http://www.

lbjlib.utexas.edu/johnson/archives.hom/speeches.hom/6405
22.asp.

3 G.W. Bush, 'The duty of hope', in M. Olasky, *Compassionate Conservatism: What It Is, What It Does, and How It Will Transform America*, Free Press, 2000.

4 D. Brooks, 'Conservatism out of balance: Eclipse of the traditionalists', *The Seattle Times*, 25 December 2012.

5 Vaclav Havel once said we 'are capable of love, friendship, solidarity, sympathy and tolerance ... we must set these fundamental dimensions of our humanity free from their "private" exile and accept them as the only genuine point of meaningful human community'. V. Havel, *The Power and the Powerless: Citizens against the State in Central Eastern Europe*, Routledge, 1985.

6 M. Sandel, *Justice: What's the Right Thing to Do?*, Penguin, 2010.

7 J. Rawls, *A Theory of Justice*, Harvard University Press, 1971.

8 C. Taylor, *The Malaise of Modernity*, House of Anansi, 1991.

9 K. Marx and F. Engels, 'Manifesto of the Communist Party', *Selected Works*, Vol. I, Progress Publishers, 1969, pp. 98–137.

10 A. Crosland, *The Future of Socialism*, Jonathan Cape, 1956.

11 R. Terrill, *R.H. Tawney and His Times: Socialism as Fellowship*, Harvard University Press, 1973.

12 For instance, in his biography of Kier Hardie, or Michael Foot, especially in the passage comparing Foot and Benn. K.O. Morgan, *Keir Hardie*, Faber and Faber, 2011; K.O. Morgan, *Michael Foot: A Life*, HarperCollins, 2008.

13 Also known as the 'Paris Manuscripts'. K. Marx and F. Engels, *Economic and Philosophic Manuscripts of 1844*, Prometheus Books, 1987.

14 Various contributions within the Frankfurt School tradition in the work of Alfred Sohn-Rethel and others have been vital in rethinking value theory away from the empirical calculations of Ricardianism towards the type of value theory of labour approach advocated here. See F.H. Pitts, *Critiquing Capitalism Today: New Ways to Read Marx*, Palgrave, 2018.

15 See E.P. Thompson, 'The poverty of theory: Or an orrery of

errors', in *The Poverty of Theory*, Monthly Review Press, 1978.

16 E.P. Thompson, *William Morris: From Romantic to Revolutionary*, Merlin Press, 1977.

17 R. Williams, *Culture and Society: 1780–1950*, Spokesman Books, 2013.

18 J. Ruskin, 'Lectures on art, 1870', in E.T. Cook and A. Wedderburn (eds), *The Works of John Ruskin*, Vol. 20, G. Allen, 1905, p. 39.

19 Ruskin the economist as well as art critic defined value: 'Valor, from valere, to be well or strong; – strong, in life (if a man), [*sic*] or valiant; strong, for life (if a thing), or valuable. To be "valuable", therefore, is to "avail towards life". A truly valuable or availing thing is that which leads to life with its whole strength. In proportion as it does not lead to life, or as its strength is broken, it is less valuable; in proportion as it leads away from life, it is unvaluable or malignant'. In Cook and Wedderburn (eds), *The Works of John Ruskin*, Vol. 17, pp. 84–5.

20 Contained in *Unto This Last*, the brilliant series of essays with his famous maxim 'there is no wealth but life' attacking the 'science' of political economy, especially Ricardo and Smith in their contraction of humanity to a 'dim-eyed and narrow-chested state of being'. J. Ruskin, *Unto This Last*, FQ Classics, 2007.

21 W. Morris, *The Hollow Land* (1856), Giniger Press, 2012.

22 See the brilliant contributions in P. Ackers and A.J. Reid (eds), *Alternatives to State-Socialism in Britain: Other Worlds of Labour in the Twentieth Century*, Palgrave Macmillan, 2016.

23 A.J. Penty, *The Restoration of the Guild System*, BiblioLife, 2009.

24 A case in point being that of the wartime social/political movement the libertarian socialist Common Wealth Party, with its expressed belief in greater morality in politics, a rejection of Fabianism and embrace of the guild tradition.

25 Ackers and Reid, *Alternatives to State-Socialism in Britain*, p. 10.

26 In the final chapter we touch on how part of this story of exile relates to the way utilitarian traditions have marginalized interest in industrial democracy across the left.

27 Especially in *Industrial Relations: What Is Wrong with the System?*, Faber, 1965; *Collective Bargaining: Selected Readings*, Penguin, 1969; and *Management and Unions: The Theory and Reform of Industrial Relations*, Faber, 1970.

28 In the 1930s, Flanders was a leading member and later the chair of the Socialist Vanguard Group and from 1934 was editor of its political magazine. This subsequently evolved into the revisionist Socialist Commentary in 1947 to rebuild a 'third way' democratic socialist philosophy. He also helped found the ethical socialist think tank Socialist Union in 1951 where he co-authored 'Socialism: A new statement of principles' (1952) and 'Twentieth century socialism' (1956), and later became a leading member of the Campaign for Democratic Socialism.

29 Kelly, *Ethical Socialism and the Trade Unions*, p. 94.

30 A.L. Blair, *A Journey*, Arrow, 2011.

31 P. Gould, *The Unfinished Revolution: How New Labour Changed British Politics for Ever*, rev. edn, Abacus, 2011.

Chapter 9: Human Labour and Radical Hope

1 In Peter Willmott's history of Dagenham (*The Evolution of a Community: A study of Dagenham After Forty Years*, Routledge and Kegan Paul, 1963), the author is struck by the continuity of attitudes with the 'traditional' working-class communities of east London such as Bethnal Green, where many Becontree residents had migrated from, and which he and Michael Young had studied in their pioneering early work (M.D. Young and P. Willmott, *Family and Kinship in East London*, Routledge and Kegan Paul, 1957).

2 J. Lear, *Radical Hope: Ethics in the Face of Cultural Devastation*, Harvard University Press, 2008.

3 C. Taylor, 'A different kind of courage', *New York Review of Books*, 26 April 2017.

4 A. Case and A. Deaton, *Deaths of Despair and the Future of Capitalism*, Princeton University Press, 2020.

5 J. Gest, *The New Minority*, Oxford University Press, 2016.

6 M. Sandel, *The Tyranny of Merit: What's Become of the Common Good*, Farrar, Straus and Giroux, 2020.

7 U. Beck, 'The cosmopolitan manifesto', *New Statesman*, 20 March 1998, pp. 38–50.

8 M. Sandel, 'Populism, Trump and the future of democracy', *Open Democracy*, 9 May 2018.

9 K. Kwarteng (ed.), *Britannia Unchained: Global Lessons for Growth and Prosperity*, Palgrave Macmillan, 2012.

10 I am indebted to Dr Stuart White of Jesus College, Oxford, for sharing his lectures notes on UBI, although he will likely disagree with my conclusions.

11 Amongst a burgeoning literature, key texts include L. Haagh, *The Case for Universal Basic Income*, Polity, 2019; H. Reed and S. Lansley, *Universal Basic Income: An Idea Whose Time Has Come?*, Compass Publications, 2016; A. Painter, 'In support of a Universal Basic Income – Introducing the RSA Basic Income Model, December 2015, RSA. https://www.thersa.org/discover/publications-and-articles/rsa-blogs/2015/12/in-support-of-a-universal-basic-income--introducing-the-rsa-basic-income-model/; G. Standing, *Basic Income as Common Dividends: Piloting a Transformative Policy*, Progressive Economy Forum, 2019; P. Van Parijs, *Basic Income: A Radical Proposal for a Free Society and a Sane Economy*, Harvard University Press, 2017.

12 Whilst we have throughout sought to rehabilitate the industrial pluralism of the Oxford School, it is worth acknowledging valid criticism of this tradition for an over-emphasis on regulations, rules and procedures rather than the democratic control of the labour process.

13 Adapted from the Institute for the Future of Work's *Good Work Charter*.

14 'Redefining Corporate Purpose: The Need to Recognise Membership Through Work', a project of Durham University Business School and the Centre for Catholic Social Thought and Practice (www.ccstp.org.uk), Ethics, Organisations and Society Research Cluster Working Paper, 17 June 2016; https://static1.squarespace.com/static/570a158d044262b3b156b18a/t/57c9a5e9f5e231c34e27e0f8/1472833007350/Recognising+Membership+Through+Work.pdf.

15 It proposed that the current categories of self-employed, employee and worker (where the definition of worker covers both employees entitled to full employment protection and people entitled to basic employment

protections), be replaced with self-employed, employee and dependent contractor. The dependent contractor category is to cover only the people entitled to basic employment protections.

16 P. Nolan, 'Good work: The Taylor Review of modern working practices', *Industrial Relations Journal*, Vol. 49, No. 5–6, 2018, pp. 400–2.

Epilogue

1 P. Mason, 'Clive Lewis and Keir Starmer are the candidates who understand how Labour must change', *New Statesman*, 8 January 2020.

Index

abstract labour, 82–4, 87, 92
accelerationism, 22, 80, 135, 157
Ackers, Peter, 146
Advisory, Conciliation and Arbitration Service (ACAS), 42, 46, 183–4
agency, 21, 86, 94, 110, 120
agency work, 128, 176
agricultural revolution, 102
Alaskan oil dividend, 23
alienation, 87, 100, 103, 112, 117, 143
Althusser, Louis, 141
Amalgamated Union of Engineering Workers (AUEW), 44–5
Angry Silence, The (1960), 31
anomie, 112
Aristotle, 131, 136, 137
Arnold, Andrea, 3, 190
artificial intelligence (AI), 2, 19–21, 126, 169
aspiration, 11, 138, 150–1
assembly-line speed, 32–3, 100, 108
asylum seekers, 154
Attenborough, Richard, 31

Attlee, Clement, 2, 38, 131, 144, 148
Auden, W.H., 144
augmented reality, 20
austerity, 18, 73, 79, 95, 158, 159, 167, 171, 187
authoritarian populism, 6, 8, 13–19, 28, 146, 158, 185
automation, 2, 11, 19–22, 36–7, 59, 79–81, 90, 92, 95, 125–9, 160, 167, 169, 171–2, 185; *see also* technological change
autonomy, 77, 100, 106, 109, 113, 122–4, 175–6, 177

Bain, George, 40
Bank of England, 25, 125, 127
Barking, 4, 97, 155, 187
Bastani, Aaron, 21
Bauman, Zygmunt, 118, 124
Beck, Ulrich, 161–2
Becontree Estate, 2, 97, 154
belonging, 7–9, 16–17
Berger, Peter, 118–19
Bevin, Ernest, 38, 147
Beynon, Huw, 100–1
Billingsgate market, 189

bioethics, 109, 110
Birmingham, 56
Blair, Tony, 4, 14, 16, 27, 40, 62–3, 68–73, 93, 136, 147–52, 156, 160, 162, 178
Blind Chance (1981), 114
Bloodworth, James, 10–12, 15, 19, 76
Booker, Cory, 23, 181
Brave New World (Huxley), 21, 108–9
Braverman, Harry, 88–9, 102, 103, 106–7, 128
Brazil, 13, 109
Brexit, 5, 17, 24, 50, 67, 73, 93, 95, 158, 165, 185–8
Brexit Party, 188
Brexit Referendum, 5, 24, 158, 188
Bridgend Engine Plant (Ford), 59, 98
Briggs Motor Bodies plant, 32, 98
Britannia Unchained, 164–5
'British disease', 27, 33, 37–41
British National Party (BNP), 2, 4, 154–5, 187–8
British Social Attitudes, 119–20
British Steel, 178
Brookes, David, 132
Brown, Gordon, 4, 62, 72–3, 134–5, 149, 160
Brown, Philip, 127–8
Brown, Willy, 40
Brynjolfsson, Erik, 19
Bullock Committee, 178
bureaucracy, 112, 113, 134, 140, 168
Burawoy, Michael, 89
Bush, George W., 110, 131–2, 137, 149

Cameron, David, 4, 132, 165, 183
Canada, 23
Capital (Marx), 85, 90, 94
capitalism, 1–2, 10–13, 27, 36–7, 53–5, 79–94, 102–9, 112–13, 124, 147, 152, 156, 169, 173
care work, 26, 74, 126, 176
Case, Anne, 156
Castells, Manuel, 93
Castle, Barbara, 3, 42–6
Catholicism, 110, 112–13, 145
Center for American Progress, 181–2
Center on Budget and Policy Priorities, 181
Centre for Engineering and Manufacturing Excellence, 72
Chaplin, Charlie, 108
Chartism, 135, 140
Child, John, 58
childcare, 23, 165
Christian Socialism, 133, 139, 144, 145
Christianity, 110, 112–13, 132–3, 136, 139, 144, 145, 149, 167
chronocentrism, 80, 160
citizenship, 2, 123, 149, 168, 170
civil rights, 132, 162
Clare, John, 104–5
Clarke, Charles, 74
class relations, 35–6, 49, 51–2, 54, 65, 81–2, 86, 87
Classical Political Economy (CPE), 27, 29, 34–7, 81–2, 91
Clegg, Hugh, 34, 146
Clinton, Bill, 14, 65
Clinton, Hillary, 23
Cobb, Jonathan, 117
Cobbett, William, 149
Cole, G.D.H., 145–6, 147
Cole, Nigel, 2–3, 43
collective bargaining, 33, 38–9, 40–1, 63, 65, 112, 146; *see also* trade unions
colonialism, 106
commodity values, 29, 35–7, 82–7, 90–1; *see also* value theory
common good, 131, 132, 137–8, 148–9, 150, 190

communism, 2, 21–2, 33, 39, 80, 92, 93, 141
Communist Manifesto (Marx & Engels), 138
community, 8–9, 15–17, 99, 103–6, 116, 118–19, 123, 131–2, 137, 156–63, 165, 170, 188
company law, 175, 178–9
Compass, 23, 170
compassionate conservatism, 131–2, 165
competition, 13, 53, 65, 76, 118
concrete labour, 36, 82–4, 87, 90–2, 94
Confederation of British Industry (CBI), 64
conservatism, 17, 49–50, 132, 164–7, 131–2, 164–7
constant capital, 83
Contribution to Political Economy, A (Marx), 85
Co-operative Society, 106
Corbyn, Jeremy, 5, 18, 76, 78, 81, 178
Corbynism, 18, 27, 63, 94, 186
corporatism, 27, 39–43, 46–7, 49, 50, 55, 64, 146, 163, 173–4
Corrosion of Character, The (Sennett), 117–18
cosmopolitanism, 16, 148, 149, 161–3, 170, 186, 188
'cost of living' framework, 134
Council on Bioethics, 110
Covid-19 pandemic
    furlough scheme, 25, 122, 163, 166, 172, 174, 182
    impacts of, 6, 12, 25–6, 122, 124–5, 158, 166–7, 172, 173–4, 176
    lockdown, 26, 122
    possible futures after, 5–6, 18, 92, 94, 95–6, 160–4, 174, 179, 182
    ventilator production in Dagenham, 2
craft, 88, 101, 115, 118
creativity, 94, 99–101, 103,
    105–6, 115, 123, 141, 143–5
Crosland, Anthony, 4, 138–9, 140, 147
Crow Indians, 156, 157
cultural death, 155–7
Culture and Society (Williams), 141–3, 145

Dagenham
    Becontree Estate, 2, 97, 154
    Brexit Referendum vote, 5, 188
    Briggs Motor Bodies plant, 32, 98
    Centre for Engineering and Manufacturing Excellence, 72
    Civic Centre, 2
    Dagenham Diesel Centre, 72, 98
    deindustrialization, 2, 154, 158–60, 187–8
    demographic change, 2, 154–5
    depicted in film, 2–5, 104, 160, 189–90
    during the Second World War, 2, 109
    family breakdown, 3
    Ford plant, 2, 3, 31–3, 43–7, 58–9, 70–2, 97–8, 100–1, 107–9, 153–4
    housing, 2, 3, 97, 154, 155, 189
    infrastructure, 97, 189
    Mardyke Estate, 3
    Michael Sandel discussion, 99–100
    munitions production, 2, 109
    regeneration, 188–9
    rise of British National Party, 2, 4, 154–5, 187–8
    strikes, 3, 33, 43–7, 59, 109
    trade unions, 31–3, 41, 43–7, 59, 71–2, 109, 153
    transport links, 97
    unemployment, 3, 59, 153–4, 159, 160
    working-class tradition, 2, 104, 154, 188

Dagenham Diesel Centre, 72, 98
Dalton, Hugh, 134, 144
Darity, William, Jr, 182
Deaton, Angus, 156
degradation, 9–13, 22, 88,
    99–101, 103–5, 110, 128,
    142, 144, 171
dehumanization, 21, 70, 105,
    107, 110, 151
deindustrialization, 2, 154,
    158–60, 187–8
Dekalog (1989), 114
Delors, Jacques, 66
democracy, 7–8, 13, 28, 68, 81,
    104, 115, 134, 135, 158; *see
    also* economic democracy;
    industrial democracy
demographic change, 2, 154–5
Denmark, 178, 183
Department of Trade and
    Industry (DTI), 72
deskilling, 88, 128
Detroit, 107–9
difference principle, 136, 168
Diggers, 138
'Digging' (Heaney), 103, 116
dignity
    and Christianity, 110, 112–13,
        149
    and creativity, 141, 143
    in Dagenham, 100–1, 104,
        159–60, 187–90
    in death, 105–6
    declarative dignity, 111, 113,
        137, 171
    decorative dignity, 111, 112,
        159
    efforts to defend and preserve,
        104–6, 144
    and human rights, 111
    nature of human dignity, 96,
        109–16, 149
    negation of, 10, 12, 110–11
    personal dignity, 111, 179–80
    and technological change,
        15–16, 106–7, 112–13, 161
    and theories of justice, 130–1,
        133, 137
    and vocation, 174, 176

work as source of, 9–10, 27,
    96, 100–1, 103, 105–6,
    112–13, 115–16, 123, 133,
    137, 141, 143, 147, 159–61,
    166, 171–4, 176, 181,
    187–90
'Dignity is a useless concept'
    (Macklin), 109
discipline, 10, 58, 108
discretion, 74, 77, 88, 100, 103,
    106, 117, 124, 175
discrimination, 46, 65, 111
dispossession, 102–6, 110, 139,
    143, 189
distributive justice, *see* wealth
    distribution
division of labour, 27, 35–7, 53,
    54
domestic labour, 89, 169
Donovan Report, 40–3, 46, 63–5
Double Life of Veronique, The
    (1991), 114
Dunlop, John, 33
Durbin, Evan, 144, 147
Durkheim, Émile, 112
'Duty of Hope, The' (Bush),
    131–2
dystopias, 2, 4, 20–1, 108, 152,
    160, 173

economic democracy, 39, 178
economic growth, 14, 17, 35–6,
    65–6, 72, 124, 130–1, 135
economic liberalism, 4, 10, 17,
    47, 62, 76, 95, 132, 142,
    149, 151–2, 159, 165
economic stimulus, 166
economism, 1, 85–6, 113, 134,
    142–3, 144, 145, 150
education, 16, 35, 70, 74–5, 76,
    134, 158, 160, 161, 176–7;
    see also training
Edwards, Richard, 89
efficient market hypothesis, 34,
    62
1844 Manuscripts, The (Marx),
    140
elections
    1970 general election, 43

1992 general election, 68
1993 Millwall byelection, 154
1994 Dagenham byelection, 154–5
1997 general election, 63, 66
2001 general election, 66
2004 Dagenham byelection, 155
2005 general election, 66, 155
2006 local elections, 155
2008 London Assembly elections, 155
2009 European elections, 155
2010 general election, 4, 187
2014 local elections, 187
2015 general election, 5, 134
2017 general election, 5, 18, 24, 185–6
2018 local elections, 187
2019 European elections, 188
2019 general election, 1, 18, 24, 166, 185–6, 187–8
  see also Brexit Referendum
embodied labour, 29, 35–7, 82, 87, 90–2, 142
Empire (Hardt & Negri), 81, 162
employee share options, 178
employment law, see labour law
Employment Protection Act, 46, 183
Employment Relations Act, 64
employment rights, 4, 38, 42, 46, 55–6, 66–7, 76, 99, 181–2, 183
enclosure, 104–5, 138
Engels, Friedrich, 86, 138
Enlightenment, 34, 112, 136
environment, 5, 20, 182
equal pay, 3, 43–4
Equal Pay Act, 43
esteem, 10, 15, 19, 99, 110, 112, 123, 163
ethical socialism, 96, 136–7, 138, 139, 144–5, 146–51
European Court of Justice, 67
European Trade Union Confederation (ETUC), 64
European Union, 5, 50, 63, 66–7, 165, 178; see also Brexit

exchange rate mechanism (ERM), 77
exchange relations, 34, 51–5, 68, 84
exchange-value, 82, 84, 142
exploitation, 12, 29, 81–3, 85–7, 104, 110, 126, 168

Fabianism, 35, 120–1, 131, 134, 139–40, 143, 144–5
Fair Wages Resolution, 55
fairness, 64, 122–3, 163–4, 180
'Fairness at Work' agenda, 64
family breakdown, 3, 4
far right, 2, 4, 65, 153, 154–5, 187–8
fascism, 39, 136, 154
fellowship, 133, 139, 144, 147
feminist theory, 89, 169
financial crisis (2008), 4, 18, 27, 50–1, 73, 76, 89, 95, 124, 159, 164
Finland, 23
Fish Tank (2009), 3–5, 104, 160, 189–90
Five Dollar Day, 108
Flanders, Allan, 34, 40, 146–7
flexible specialization, 70
flexible working, 67, 120, 128, 166
focus groups, 68
forced labour, 106
Ford, Edsel, 98
Ford, Henry, 107–9
Ford, Martin, 20, 23
Ford plant, Dagenham, 2, 3, 31–3, 43–7, 58–9, 70–2, 97–8, 100–1, 107–9, 153–4
Ford plant, Detroit, 107–9
Ford plant, Halewood, 44, 45, 100
Fordism, 3, 70, 88, 103, 107–8, 188
Fourier, Charles, 138
Fowles, Jib, 80
Fragment on Machines (Marx), 90–1, 93–4
France, 138, 179
franchise, 104, 105

Francis, Bill, 33
Francis, Pope, 110, 113
Free Enterprise Group, 165
freedom models of justice, 96,
    133, 135–6
Frey, Carl, 20, 125–7
Friedman, Andrew L., 89
Friedman, Milton, 22, 169
furlough scheme, 25, 122, 163,
    166, 172, 174, 182
Future of Socialism, The
    (Crosland), 4, 138–9, 140
Future of the Professions, The
    (Susskind & Susskind), 20
Future of Work Commission, 175

Gaitskell, Hugh, 144
Galbraith, J.K., 22, 51
gender, 3, 43–4, 46, 89, 165,
    169, 176
General Enclosure Act, 104
Germany, 14, 39, 178, 183
Giant's Strength, A, 39, 47
Giddens, Tony, 40
gig economy, 128, 183
Gillibrand, Kirsten, 23, 181
globalization, 4, 8, 63, 65, 69,
    81, 95, 137, 156, 161–3
good work, 73, 100, 123, 165–6,
    172, 175–6; *see also* job
    quality
Gorz, André, 128
Gould, Bryan, 155
Gould, Philip, 150–1
Government Communication
    Headquarters (GCHQ), 56
Graeber, David, 22
Greek civilization, 106
Green New Deal, 182
Griffin, Nick, 4, 187
Guardian, 91
Guild Socialism, 139, 145–6
Gunter, Ray, 42

Haagh, Louise, 171
Halewood, 44, 45, 100
Hall, Stuart, 4, 146
Hamilton, Darrick, 182
Hardie, Keir, 131, 144

Hardt, Michael, 81, 162
Harvard GoodWork Project,
    175
Harvey, David, 8
Hayek, F.A., 22
health, *see* healthcare; mental
    health; physical health
Health and Safety Executive
    (HSE), 42
healthcare, 5, 23, 181
Heaney, Seamus, 103, 116
Heath, Edward, 43, 46
Hidden Injuries of Class, The
    (Sennett & Cobb), 117
hierarchical structures, 58, 69
higher education, 74–5, 134, 161,
    176–7
Hired (Bloodworth), 10–12, 15,
    19, 76
Hodge, Margaret, 155
Hodgkiss, Philip, 111–12
holiday pay, 180
home, working from, 26, 180
Hoskins, Bob, 3
Hoskyns, John, 48
hour glass economy, 74–5
housework, 89, 169
housing, 2, 3, 23, 97, 154, 155,
    166, 181, 189
Howe, Geoffrey, 116
human capital, 16, 70, 128
Human Dignity and Bioethics
    (Council on Bioethics), 110
Human Relations School, 58
Human Resource Management,
    58, 59, 89
human rights, 22, 109–10, 111,
    113, 135–6, 149, 168, 181–2
Human Rights Act, 136
humanism, 4, 21, 85, 96, 110,
    113–16, 139, 140–1, 147,
    151, 190
Hume, Basil, 149
humiliation, 11, 14, 19, 100,
    110, 117, 159, 160, 163–4
Hungary, 13
hunter-gatherer societies, 102
Hutton, Will, 124
Huxley, Aldous, 21, 108–9

identity, 9, 11, 28, 99, 100, 104, 106, 115, 123, 162
I'm All Right Jack (1959), 31–2
immigration, 154–5
In Place of Strife White Paper, 43, 44–6
Independent Labour Party (ILP), 131, 139–40, 143, 144–5
individualism, 24, 151, 152, 162
industrial democracy, 24, 139, 145, 166, 174, 178–9
industrial relations, 3, 26–7, 29, 31–4, 38–47, 55–9, 64, 71–2, 109, 146–7
Industrial Relations Act, 41, 43, 46
Industrial Relations Commission, 41–2
Industrial Relations Court, 46
Industrial Revolution, 19–20, 102, 104, 142
industrial sociology, 29, 70, 88
'Industrial Strategy' White Paper, 127
inequality, 14–15, 19–20, 56, 136, 158, 160, 168, 171
infrastructure, 97, 166, 174, 181, 189
initiative-taking, 77, 120, 124, 175
'Insecure Work' report, 121
Institute for Public Policy Research (IPPR), 121
intangible assets, 69–70
International Covenant of Economic, Social and Cultural Rights, 181
International Labour Organization (ILO), 181
International Monetary Fund (IMF), 170
Ipsos MORI, 120–1
Italy, 13, 80–1, 90

Japan, 59
Jay, Douglas, 144
Jenkins, Roy, 4, 136
job guarantees, 23, 99, 170, 172, 181–2

job insecurity, 9, 10, 23, 112, 118, 120–4, 128, 176, 180; *see also* precarious employment
job quality, 120–5, 165–6; *see also* good work
job satisfaction, 119–21
job security, 23, 119–22
John Paul II, 112–13, 114
Johnson, Boris, 17, 149, 166–7, 188
Johnson, Lyndon, 22, 131, 137, 149
Jones, Jack, 2, 44–6
Joseph, Keith, 50
justice, theories of, 1, 4, 7, 12, 26–8, 76, 96, 130–40, 147, 169, 187

Kautsky, Karl, 85
Kennedy, Bobby, 130–1, 137, 149
Keynes, John Maynard, 125
Keynesianism, 166
Kieslowski, Krzysztof, 113–16, 133
Kirby Engineering, 178
'Knowledge-Based Economy' White Paper, 70
knowledge economy, 69–70, 74–5
knowledge work, 16, 63, 69–70, 74–5, 80, 128, 160, 177
Korsch, Karl, 54
Kwarteng, Kwasi, 164

Laborem Exercens, 112–13, 114
Labour and Monopoly Capitalism (Braverman), 88–9, 102, 103, 106–7, 128
labour courts, 43, 44
Labour Force Survey (LFS), 73, 121
labour law, 38–43, 46, 55–6, 64–7, 71, 128, 175, 183
labour market segmentation, 89, 122, 123, 124, 169
labour power, 83–4, 87–9

labour process theory, 88–9,
    106–7
labour regulation, 26–9, 38–43,
    48–50, 62–9, 76–9, 87,
    105–6, 126, 145–7, 160,
    174, 183–4
labour relations, *see* industrial
    relations
Labour revisionism, 4, 146, 147
labour theory of value (Marxist),
    82–7, 90–1, 107, 186
labour theory of value
    (Ricardian), 35–7, 54, 82,
    84, 87, 90–1
labour tribunals, 42
labourism, 4, 174
laissez-faire economics, 51–2
laissez-faire regulation, 38, 40
Laker, Alfred, 148
Lansbury, George, 2, 131, 144
Laski, Harold, 146
law, *see* company law; labour law
Leadbeater, Charles, 69–70, 93,
    160
Lear, Jonathan, 155–7, 189
Lee, Bernard, 31
Lenin, Vladimir, 107
Leo XIII, 112
Levellers, 135
liberal democracy, 7–8, 13, 18,
    28, 158
liberalism, *see* economic
    liberalism; neo-liberalism;
    political liberalism; Radical
    Liberalism
living standards, 66, 77
living wage, 112, 166, 176, 182
lockdown, 26, 122
London, 32, 97, 108–9, 189; *see
    also* Dagenham
London Development Agency,
    72
Longbridge, 71, 72
low-paid jobs, 10, 74, 119, 121,
    122, 125, 165, 176, 180
Low Pay Commission, 40, 64
Lucas Aerospace,
    178
luxury communism, 2, 22, 80, 92

McAfee, Andrew, 19
McCartney, Ian, 40, 64
MacDonald, Ramsay, 131, 144
McDonnell, John, 23, 170
McEwan, Ian, 21
McKinsey Global, 125, 126
Machines Like Me (McEwan), 21
Macklin, Ruth, 109
Macmillan, Harold, 39
Macmurray, John, 148
Made in Dagenham (2010), 2–4,
    31, 43, 104, 160
Malthus, Thomas, 34
Manchester, 97
Manitoba Mincome project, 23
Manpower Services Commission
    (MSC), 42, 55
marginalism, 51–3
market economy, 8, 14, 17, 19,
    34, 51–4, 62, 85, 105, 135,
    152, 165
Marx, Karl, 27, 79, 81–94, 106,
    112, 135, 138–41, 186
Marxism, 8, 22, 29, 79–94,
    106–7, 135, 140–5, 162,
    168, 185
Mason, Paul, 22, 37, 90–1, 93,
    128, 185–6
mass production, 3, 107, 129
materialism, 85–6, 115, 140–1,
    147
maternity leave, 67, 166
May, Theresa, 23–4, 165–6,
    180
May Day Manifesto, The
    (Williams, Thompson &
    Hall), 4
meaningful work, 11, 96, 99,
    143, 147; *see also* good
    work; job quality
meaningless work, 9, 22, 103
mechanization, 20, 58, 113, 142;
    see also automation
media, 19, 20, 63, 72, 154, 155,
    164–5
mediating structures, 118–19
mental health, 3, 121, 122, 123,
    166, 176
Meriden Motorcycles, 178

meritocracy, 15–16, 70, 117, 156, 161, 164
Metal, Stamping and Body (MSB) plant (Ford), 98
migration, 126, 154–5, 170–1
Miliband, Ed, 134
Mill, J. S., 34, 139
Millwall, 154
Milne-Bailey, Walter, 146
miners' strikes, 46, 56
minimum wage, 64, 134, 183
Mishra, Pankaj, 13
modern slavery, 183
Modern Times (1936), 108
Momentum organization, 81
Monks, John, 40, 64
Mores, The (Clare), 104–5
Morgan, Ken, 131, 139–40
Morris, William, 133, 139, 141–4, 145, 147, 148, 149
Murray, Charles, 22, 169
My Life and Work (Ford), 108

Nasser, Jack, 71
nation, 8, 16–17, 131, 132, 148–9, 162–3, 165
National Board for Prices and Incomes, 42
National Economic Development Council (NEDC), 39, 42, 55
National Enterprise Board (NEB), 42, 55
National Front, 154
National Guilds League, 145
National Joint Negotiating Committee (NJNC), 32, 41, 43, 45, 59
National Living Wage, 166
National Minimum Wage Act, 64
National Union of Mineworkers (NUM), 56
nationalism, 171, 185, 186, 187
natural law, 113, 139
Nazism, 111
Negri, Antonio, 81, 90–1, 162
Nelson, Leonard, 146
Neo-Classical Economics, 27, 29, 47, 48, 50–5, 61, 70, 86, 135

neo-liberalism, 2, 8, 17–19, 29, 34, 50, 62, 80, 116, 135, 137, 159, 182
Netherlands, 23
networked youth, 91–3, 161, 162, 186
Neuhaus, Richard John, 118–19
New Age, 145
New Deal, 23
New Economics Foundation, 121
New Fabian Research Bureau, 144
New Labour, 4, 16, 27, 40, 62–80, 134–5, 148–52, 154, 159–60, 162, 186
New Left, 4, 141–2, 145, 146
New Right, 14, 27, 62, 79
New Society, 39
New Spitalfields market, 189
New Statesman, 93
New Zealand, 23, 183
Nineteen Eighty-Four (Orwell), 21
Nixon, Richard, 22
Notes Toward the Definition of Policy (Joseph), 50

Obama, Barack, 5, 14, 23, 109–10, 137
Occupy movement, 81
Office for National Statistics (ONS), 25
Olasky, Marvin, 131–2
Organisation for Economic Co-operation and Development (OECD), 126, 170
Orwell, George, 21
Osborne, George, 178, 183
Osborne, Mike, 20, 125–7
Owen, Robert, 138, 139, 149
Oxford School, 34, 39–40, 42, 46, 96, 146–7

Paine, Tom, 22, 135, 140, 168
Paint Trim and Assembly (PTA) plant (Ford), 33, 98
parental leave, 67, 166
Parliamentary Reform Act, 105
part-time work, 121

Patel, Priti, 164
paternalism, 139
paternity leave, 67, 166
patriarchy, 89
paupers, 104–6
paupers' graves, 105–6
pay, *see* wages
Penty, Arthur, 145
perfect competition, 53
personal data, 179–80
physical health, 100, 115, 122, 123, 166, 176
physical labour, 36, 70, 101–3
pickets, 56, 76
Pinker, Steven, 110
Piore, Michael, 70, 93
Plato, 157
Plekhanov, Georgi, 85
pluralism, 27, 33–4, 36, 39–42, 47, 63–6, 76, 79, 93, 95, 145–6
Poland, 13, 113–16
Polanyi, Karl, 105, 146
political liberalism, 13, 15, 16, 17–18, 50, 135–6
Poor Law Reform Act, 105
Popular Fronts, 85
populism, 6, 8, 13–19, 28, 146, 158, 160, 163–4, 185, 188
Post Office, 178
postcapitalism, 2, 22, 27, 79, 80–1, 90–3, 135
PostCapitalism (Mason), 22, 90–1, 185
post-Fordism, 107
post-work theories, 2, 6, 16, 19–23, 27, 80–1, 92–3, 128, 135, 160, 171–2, 187
post-workerism (*postoperaismo*), 80–1, 135, 187
pragmatism, 23–5, 144, 162
precarious employment, 9, 95, 100, 118, 128, 129, 180; *see also* job insecurity
Prior Act, 55
private labour, 82–4
privatization, 62, 178
production, 34–7, 52–4, 70, 81–94, 100–1, 135, 168

productivity
  drivers of, 124–5, 175
  UK productivity levels, 24–5, 27, 37–41, 60–1, 76–7, 79, 94, 95, 125, 166, 172
  worker productivity, 42, 45, 52–3, 89, 107, 184
professional occupations, 20, 119, 127
Protestant work ethic, 106
Public Philosopher series (BBC), 99
public sector strikes, 47
public services, 18, 62, 66, 72–3, 165, 168, 169, 172
PwC, 125, 127

quality circles, 59

Raab, Dominic, 164
Race Relations Act, 46
radical hope, 155–7, 187, 189–90
Radical Liberalism, 135
Ragged Trousered Philanthropists, The (Tressell), 105
rationality, 27, 52–5, 139, 144
Rawls, John, 136, 140, 168
Reagan, Ronald, 14
reciprocity, 106, 123, 132–3, 138, 169
'Red Wall', 5, 17, 24, 166, 188
redundancies, 59, 71–2, 184
regulation, *see* labour regulation
religion, 106, 110, 112–13, 132–3, 136–7, 141–5, 149–50
Report of the Future of Work Commission, 175
Rerum Novarum, 112
resentment, 5, 14–15, 18, 163–4, 188
Resolution Foundation, 121–2
Restoration of the Guild System (Penty), 145
Ricardianism, 35–7, 54, 82, 84, 87, 90–1, 135, 168, 174
Ricardo, David, 34–7, 79, 82, 84, 87, 90–1, 139

Richardson, Miranda, 3
Rifkin, Jeremy, 128
rights, *see* civil rights;
    employment rights; human
    rights
'Rights for Whites' campaign,
    154
Robinson, Joan, 147
Roman civilization, 106
Romanticism, 112, 141, 145
Roosevelt, Franklin D., 181
Rover plant, Longbridge, 71, 72
Royal Society for Arts,
    Manufactures and
    Commerce (RSA), 170
Ruskin, John, 142, 145
Russell, Bertrand, 22
Russia, 13, 85, 107

Sable, Chuck, 70, 93
Sainsbury Report, 176–7
Sakar, Ash, 21
Saltley Gate, 56
Sandel, Michael, 13–16, 18–19,
    99–100, 118, 163–4
Sanders, Bernie, 23, 181
Scanlon, Hugh, 44–6
scarcity, 35, 52, 87
Scheele, Nick, 71
Schröder, Gerhard, 14
Schumpeter, Joseph, 68
science fiction, 21
Scientific Management, 57–8, 88,
    101, 103, 107
Scotland, 23
Scottish Daily Express, 178
Searchlight, 153
Second International, 85, 140
Second World War, 2, 38, 109,
    146
self-employment, 73, 121, 128,
    182
self-realization, 103, 143, 144,
    173
Sellers, Peter, 31–2
Sennett, Richard, 117–18, 124
service sector, 74, 75, 126
Sessions, John, 3
Sex Discrimination Act, 46

shareholder value, 179
sick pay, 180
Skidmore, Chris, 164
Skills and Employment Survey,
    77, 124, 128–9, 175
slavery, 106, 111, 183
slum clearances, 2
Smith, Adam, 34–7, 82, 159
Smith, John, 64
Smithfield market, 189
social contract theory, 136, 171
social democracy, 1, 5, 14,
    17–19, 28–9, 80, 95, 116,
    134, 136, 146, 147, 179
Social Democratic Federation
    (SDF), 144
social housing, 2, 3, 154, 155
social labour, 82–3, 87
social mobility, 9, 14
social partnership, 64
social realism, 4, 114
socialism, 4, 28, 49, 50, 89, 93,
    96, 104, 106, 133, 136,
    138–51
socialist humanism, 4, 85, 96,
    147
solidarity, 3, 11, 131, 137
Solidarity movement, 114, 116
Stalinism, 85, 136
Standing, Guy, 23
state intervention, 25, 51, 62,
    64–6, 68, 173–4
Stepping Stones report, 48–50,
    55, 164
Strauss, Norman S., 48
stress, 99, 120, 122
strikes, 3, 33, 38, 41, 42, 43–7,
    55–6, 59, 72, 76, 109
structuralism, 85, 140–1
subjective preferences, 34, 51–2,
    54–5
suggestion-making, 77, 124,
    175
Sun, 63
supply chains, 175, 179, 183
supply-side reform, 27, 55, 61,
    62, 72, 95
Sure Start agenda, 149
surplus value, 83, 85, 87, 92

surveillance (of workers), 10, 179–80
Susskind, Daniel, 20
Susskind, Richard, 20
Sweden, 183
syndicalism, 139
Systems Theory, 33–4

Taff Vale judgment, 38
Talking Heads (Gadaj⬛ce Głowy) (1980), 114–16, 133
task fragmentation, 58, 88
Tawney, R. H., 139, 145, 146, 148, 149
tax credits, 66, 72–3, 134, 159, 160
taxation, 49, 63, 66, 68, 72–3, 134, 165, 167, 169
Taylor, Charles, 138
Taylor, F.W., 58, 101
Taylor, Matthew, 24
Taylor Review, 24, 165, 175, 180, 184
Taylorism, 57–8, 59, 88, 101, 103, 128, 129
Tebbitt Act, 55
technocracy, 1, 14, 18, 80, 134, 160
technological change
  and determinism, *see* technological determinism
  and dignity, 15–16, 106–7, 112–13, 161
  disruptive effects of, 8, 15–16, 19–21, 125–9
  and knowledge work, 16, 69–70, 80, 128, 160
  and Marxism, 82, 84–6, 88–95, 106–7, 186
  and neo-classical theory, 53–4
  and networked youth, 91–3, 161, 162, 186
  and post-work theories, 2, 6, 16, 19–23, 27, 80–1, 92–3, 96, 128, 135, 160, 171–2, 187
  and unemployment, 15–16, 20, 22–3, 69, 112, 125–7, 171–2
  and universal basic income,
  16, 22–3, 80, 92, 160, 169, 171–2
  and utopianism, 1–2, 6, 16, 19, 21–2, 27, 80–1, 86, 107, 138, 146, 162, 169–70, 173
  and value theory, 82, 84–6, 90–4, 107, 186
  see also automation
technological determinism, 22, 27, 76, 86, 89–94, 125–9, 156–7, 160–2, 164, 171–2, 186–7
temporary work, 121
Thatcher, Margaret, 14, 17, 24, 27, 47, 49–50, 58, 63, 73, 95, 116, 148, 164, 178
Thatcherism, 29, 47, 50, 60–1, 66, 166
Theory of Justice, A (Rawls), 136
Third Way politics, 5, 17–18, 40, 94, 161–2
30/30/40 society, 124
Thompson, E.P., 4, 141–2, 145
Three Colours trilogy (1993–4), 114, 133
Todd, Ron, 2, 59, 153–4
Tomlinson Commission, 177
top 1% (wealth of), 56–7
totalitarianism, 21, 114, 141, 146
Trade Disputes Act, 38, 56
Trade Union and Labour Relations Act (TULRA), 46
trade unions
  attacks on power of, 49–50, 55–7
  ballot regulations, 43
  and collective bargaining, 33, 38–9, 40–1, 63, 65, 112, 146
  and the Covid-19 pandemic, 166
  in Dagenham, 31–3, 41, 43–7, 59, 71–2, 109, 153
  and the Donovan Report, 40–3, 46, 64–5
  emergence of general unions, 31
  immunity from prosecution, 38
  and industrial democracy, 178
  and job guarantees, 182

membership levels, 56–7, 75–6
militancy of, 68
recognition of, 32, 41–2, 43,
    46, 56, 64–5, 99, 109, 183
reform of, 39
response to Taylor Review, 24
restrictions upon, 55–6
shop steward power, 33, 41,
    42–3, 44
and the *Stepping Stones* report,
    49–50
and unofficial action, 31, 32–3,
    39, 42, 43, 45–6, 56
Trades Union Congress (TUC),
    40, 42, 45–6, 59, 64, 66,
    121, 127, 146–7, 163,
    173–4
training, 65, 71, 158, 176–7,
    182, 184, 189; *see also*
    education
Transport and General Workers'
    Union (TGWU), 44–5, 59,
    153
Treasury, 25, 63, 65–6, 72, 76,
    150, 159–60
Tressell, Robert, 105
Trinity Formula, 35, 55
True Levellers, 138
Trump, Donald, 132, 158
Truss, Liz, 164
Turkey, 13
Tyndall, John, 154–5

UK Independence Party (UKIP),
    155, 18
unemployment, 3, 20, 22–3,
    25–6, 56, 59, 112, 122,
    153–4, 159–60, 171–2
unfair dismissal, 42, 46, 64
Unfinished Revolution, The
    (Gould), 150–1
Union Modernisation Fund, 65
unitarism, 57–9, 61
United Nations Economic and
    Social Council (ECOSOC),
    175
United Nations Special
    Rapporteur on poverty,
    170

United States, 13, 14, 23, 25, 37,
    65, 70, 107–10, 130–2, 137,
    156, 158, 181–2
universal basic income (UBI), 16,
    22–3, 28, 80, 92, 99, 159,
    160, 167–74, 182
Universal Credit, 25, 170
Universal Declaration of Human
    Rights, 111, 136, 181
use-value, 82–4, 92
utilitarianism, 1, 4, 21, 28, 36,
    65, 94, 108, 134–9, 142–5,
    149–52, 158–60, 164,
    167–8, 174, 178
utopianism, 1–2, 6, 16, 19, 21–2,
    27, 80–1, 86, 107, 138, 146,
    162, 169–70, 173

value theory, 27, 35–7, 51, 54,
    79, 81–7, 90–4, 139, 142,
    185
Van Parijs, Philippe, 171
variable capital, 83
virtue, 96, 132, 133, 136–8,
    139–44, 169
vocation, 9, 115–16, 137, 166,
    174, 176–7
vocational qualifications, 176–7
voice, 77, 124, 177–9
Voice of Ford Workers, 32
Volkswagen emissions scandal,
    98
voluntarism, 38–9, 40–1, 43, 46,
    55–6, 63, 66

wages
  and collective bargaining, 33,
    38–9, 40–1, 63, 65, 112, 146
  declines in, 65, 159
  equal pay, 3, 43–4
  fair pay, 55, 123, 175
  Fair Wages Resolution, 55
  and gender, 3, 43–4
  living wage, 112, 166, 176,
    182
  low-paid jobs, 10, 74, 119,
    121, 122, 125, 165, 176,
    180
  Low Pay Commission, 40, 64

wages (*cont.*)
  and marginalism, 53
  minimum wage, 64, 134, 183
  poverty pay, 149, 169
  real wages, 60, 65, 159
  rises in, 60
  stagnation of, 73, 77, 79, 128, 134–5, 169
  strikes for better pay, 3, 43–7
  and surplus value, 83
  wage drift, 39, 42
  wages councils, 38, 55
  well-paid jobs, 23, 119, 120
Walden, Brian, 49
Warwick School, 34
Watson, Tom, 175
wealth distribution, 1, 15, 27, 34–6, 54–7, 62, 72, 87, 134–5, 139, 158–9, 168, 174, 188
Weber, Max, 112
welfare models of justice, 96, 133, 134–5, 139–40
welfare state, 14, 22, 25, 68, 72, 76, 158–60, 165, 169, 170, 172
Wells, H.G., 21
Welsh Development Agency, 59
whistle-blowers, 64
Why I am a Christian (Blair), 149
Williams, Raymond, 4, 141–3, 145
Wilson, Harold, 3, 4, 39, 42–6, 178
Winstanley, Gerrard, 138
Wordsworth, Dorothy, 104

Wordsworth, William, 104
work, defining, 101–3
work assessment forums, 183–4
work ethic, 106, 165
work intensification, 61, 73, 106, 120, 123, 124
work–life balance, 67
worker cooperatives, 178
worker directors, 178, 179
Worker Ownership Funds, 178
workerist movement (*operaismo*), 80
workhouses, 105, 106
Working for Ford (Beynon), 100–1
working hours, 26, 66, 67, 74, 77, 99, 106, 125, 165
Working Time Directive, 66
'Workington Man', 24, 166
Workplace Employment Relations Study (WERS), 183, 184
works councils, 178, 179, 184
Works Progress Administration, 181
worth, 9, 18, 110, 117, 163

XYZ Group, 144

Yang, Andrew, 23
YouGov, 119
Young, Michael, 146
Youngstown, OH, 158

zero-hours contracts, 121, 128, 166, 176, 180